Renato Henrique Rehder

Penal age

Renato Henrique Rehder

Penal age

Child and adolescent crime

ScienciaScripts

Cover image: www.ingimage.com

This book is a translation from the original published under ISBN 978-3-330-76295-4.

Publisher:
Sciencia Scripts
is a trademark of
Dodo Books Indian Ocean Ltd. and OmniScriptum S.R.L publishing group

120 High Road, East Finchley, London, N2 9ED, United Kingdom
Str. Armeneasca 28/1, office 1, Chisinau MD-2012, Republic of Moldova, Europe
Managing Directors: Ieva Konstantinova, Victoria Ursu
info@omniscriptum.com

Printed at: see last page
ISBN: 978-620-8-40329-4

To my parents and brother,
for their love and support.

ACKNOWLEDGEMENTS

To God, for giving me an extraordinary family and for his daily protection, even when I was travelling.

To my parents, Francisco Carlos Rehder Filho and Silvia Fátima Alves Rehder, for their mutual affection and unconditional love. To my father, for his example of honesty, honour and simplicity. To my mother, for being my companion, counsellor and for always being willing to help with a lot of affection and love.

To my brother Francisco Carlos Rehder Neto, for his example of dedication and determination. I'm very proud to be your brother and to be able to share our achievements.

To my "sister-in-law" Janaína Castania, for her friendship, affection and support over all these years. I found in you the sister I never had.

To Gabriela, for her constant encouragement on the importance of professional and academic updating, including her patience and affection.

To my aunts "Lu", "Bete" and godmother Rose, for their care, love and attention over the years. My cousins Larissa, for their friendship, affection and company, and Melissa for her happiness and contagious sweetness.

To my "brothers in heart": "Beto", Eduardo and Luciano, for their company and friendship.

To my uncles "Zé" and "Carlos" for turning weekends into real parties.

To my godmother Ana and my godfather José, for their love, friendship and affection.

To my friends: Guilherme, Leandro, Neves, Fabinho, Sandra, Karen, "Manu" and Mônica for their friendship and companionship. I thank God for having put you in my life.

To my friend Naul Luiz Felca, for the teachings that I will carry with me throughout my professional life. Thank you for your support and encouragement in my choices.

To my teachers who took part in my academic training, true masters, without whom it would not have been possible to realise this dream. Many thanks to all of you.

To my teacher and supervisor Marisa Helena D'arbo Alves de Freitas, for her attention, promptness and encouragement. I've learnt a lot from you over the years. Thank you very much!

To my teacher and supervisor Regina Claudia Laisner, who was responsible for shaping me as a researcher and teacher. I would like to thank her for her attention over the last few years and for her constant encouragement to research. Thank you very much!

Finally, I couldn't fail to pay homage to the people who, unfortunately, have already been called by God, but whom I remember with great affection and love: my grandfathers Matemos Oliveira and Maria, my paternal grandfathers Chico and Lídia, my unforgettable aunt Nadir and my dear godfather Bastião and godmother Ana. You're all very much missed. I love you all.

"The really good thing is to go into battle with determination, embrace life with passion, lose with class and win with daring, because the world belongs to those who dare and life is too much to be insignificant. " Augusto Branco

SUMMARY

The growing number of offences committed by children and adolescents is a problem that is getting worse every day and various proposals have been discussed with a view to finding a solution, including reducing the age of criminal responsibility. There has been speculation about lowering the age limit set by the country's legislature, as well as a study of the procedures to be adopted with the aim of adapting the socio-educational measures introduced by the Statute of the Child and Adolescent, measures that are applied to adolescent offenders and which are both punitive and re-socialising. There is much discussion about improvements to be made, or a possible replacement of the model adopted. The purpose of this study is to analyse the issue of child and adolescent crime and the age of criminal responsibility in Brazil in accordance with the age set by the legislation in force, by analysing the legislation of other countries, as well as examining the procedure established in the Statute of the Child and Adolescent for the investigation of the offence and the application of the socio-educational measure.

KEY WORDS: age of criminal responsibility, adolescent offenders, socio-educational measures.

SUMMARY

INTRODUCTION

Child and adolescent crime has increased significantly over the years, and the participation of children and adolescents in criminal activities has become commonplace. However, the false idea has been created that no measures are taken to hold adolescent offenders criminally responsible, a fact that does not correspond to reality, but which generates a feeling of impunity in society.

Brazil has an internationally acclaimed juvenile legislation that regulates the investigation of offences, the procedure for socio-educational action, as well as socio-educational measures. It was therefore up to the Statute of the Child and Adolescent to regulate the special treatment given to children and adolescents when the current Federal Constitution was enacted.

The Brazilian legal system, in line with international treaties on the subject, sets the age of criminal majority at eighteen, given that young people are in full physical and mental development until they reach this age and therefore need to be treated differently.

From this perspective, a discussion arises about the problem of child and adolescent crime and the maintenance or alteration of the model of criminal responsibility, which is the subject of this study.

The first chapter, entitled "Child and Adolescent Violence, Procedure and Socio-Educational Measures Regulated by the Statute of the Child and Adolescent", addressed issues relating to child and adolescent crime, analysing the number of offences committed in each state of the Federation, which provided a macro view of the problem. Next, the history of Brazilian legislation for children and adolescents was analysed, from the colonial period to the current Statute of the Child and Adolescent, when a study was made of the investigation of offences, the procedure for socio-educational action, as well as socio-educational measures and their purpose.

The second chapter, on "Criminal Majority, Criteria for its Establishment and Comparative Law", initially established a relationship between age and criminal majority, addressing the criteria used by the legislator to establish the starting age for criminal responsibility at eighteen years of age. It also reflected on the treatment adopted in other countries, comparing foreign legislation with Brazilian legislation, including a case study.

The third chapter dealt with "Penal Majority: Reduction, Maintenance or Alteration of the Paradigm Adopted by the Brazilian State", questioning whether or not the age set by the country's legislature for holding young people criminally responsible when they commit criminal offences should be altered. The article presents doctrinal currents in favour of a possible paradigm shift and those against, which advocate maintaining the current model by maintaining the age of criminal majority at eighteen.

The aim of this work was to study the problem of offences committed by children and adolescents and, in this way, by analysing child and adolescent crime and the relevant legislation, it was possible to address controversial issues such as lowering the starting age for criminal responsibility and the criteria used to establish it, while also analysing foreign legal systems to gain a better understanding of the institute.

To this end, the dogmatic-legal and deductive methods were used, valuing the positive norms, as well as the historical and comparative process through which the institute studied was understood. These methods proved to be effective, given that this is a controversial issue, which will be understood through comparative study between different systems.

CHAPTER 1

CHILD AND ADOLESCENT VIOLENCE, PROCEDURE AND SOCIO-EDUCATIONAL MEASURES REGULATED BY THE STATUTE OF THE CHILD AND ADOLESCENT

1.1 Child and youth violence

One of the problems that directly affects society and is reported daily in the media is violence, which manifests itself in a wide variety of forms, such as domestic violence, violence against property, violence resulting from illegal drug trafficking, among others[1] . What is striking is that children and adolescents are becoming more and more involved in these practices.

This is the issue that is the subject of this study, a topic that, more often than not, is not discussed or addressed in the way it should be by society. Tânia da Silva Pereira says that "[...] juvenile delinquency is a social phenomenon that demands fair responses, and these cannot persist based on myths, euphemisms and fallacies."[2]

Paulo Lúcio Nogueira adds that "[...] the problem of minors remains a priority only in lectures, meetings, congresses, on the eve of elections [...], as if that were enough to solve the problem."[3] The author also believes that "[...] we have felt that juvenile delinquency has been increasing precisely because of this social indifference to the problems of minors, always prioritised by our authorities, but never tackled with due seriousness."[4]

The National Survey of Socio-educational Assistance to Adolescents in Conflict with the Law for 2010[5] , carried out by the National Secretariat for the Promotion of the Rights of Children and Adolescents, shows the scale of the current problem involving violence against children and adolescents.

The study shows that the number of adolescents deprived of their liberty in the Brazilian socio-educational system increased significantly between 1996 and 2010. The data shows that the number of adolescents serving a socio-educational measure involving deprivation of liberty went from just over four thousand two hundred to almost eighteen thousand, an increase of over four hundred percent in the period analysed.

---

[1] See Annex I.

[2] PEREIRA, Tânia da Silva. **Direito da criança e do adolescente:** uma proposta interdisciplinar. 2. ed. rev. e atual. Rio de Janeiro: Renovar. 2008. p. 994.

[3] NOGUEIRA, Paulo Lúcio. **Comentários ao código de menores.** 3 ed. São Paulo: Saraiva. 1987. p. IX.

[4] Ibid., p. XIV.

[5] NATIONAL SURVEY OF SOCIO-EDUCATIONAL CARE FOR ADOLESCENTS IN CONFLICT WITH THE LAW 2010. Available at: <http://www.viablog.org.br/conteudo/LEVANTAMENTO_Socioed.pdf>. Accessed on: 9 July 2011. Annex II.

The table below[6] shows, in official figures, the high growth that took place between 1996 and 2010.

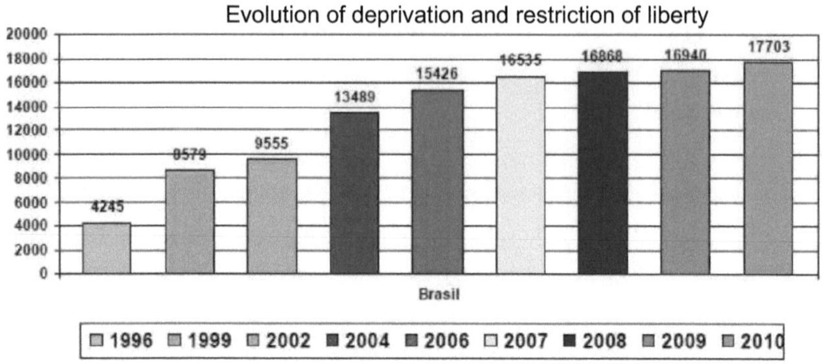

The table above shows that in the last four years the rate of increase had fallen, but between 2009 and 2010 there was a new increase in the rates. This shows that the number of offences committed by adolescents has increased, especially those considered serious, since these are usually the ones that lead to deprivation of liberty.

It is important to note that in 2010 in Brazil, the state of São Paulo, the most populous in the country, with an estimated population of more than 41 million people[7] , had more than a third of the total number of young people deprived of their liberty. This doesn't mean that this state has the highest number of children and adolescents involved in illegal practices; on the contrary, the joint efforts of the police, the Public Prosecutor's Office and the Judiciary in the fight against child crime should be emphasised.

In a different position, Rio de Janeiro, the third most populous state in the country, with an estimated population of almost sixteen million[8] , which has high rates of violence and problems related to the illicit trafficking of narcotic substances, as is reported daily in the media, has just over six hundred young people deprived of their liberty.

In accordance with the National Survey of Socio-Educational Assistance for 2010[9] , it can

---

[6] **NATIONAL SURVEY OF SOCIO-EDUCATIONAL CARE FOR ADOLESCENTS IN CONFLICT WITH THE LAW 2010.** Available at: <http://www.viablog.org.br/conteudo/LEVANTAMENTO_Socioed.pdf>. Accessed on: 9 July 2011.

[7] BRAZILIAN INSTITUTE OF GEOGRAPHY AND STATISTICS. **Channels:** States@: São Paulo. Available at <http://www.ibge.gov.br/estadosat/perfil.php?sigla=sp>. Accessed on 07 May 2011.

[8] BRAZILIAN INSTITUTE OF GEOGRAPHY AND STATISTICS. **Population.** 2010 Census. Available at: <http://www.ibge.gov.br/home/presid.encia/noticias/noticia_visualiza.php?id_noticia=1766>. Accessed on 07 May 2011.

[9] **NATIONAL SURVEY OF SOCIO-EDUCATIONAL CARE FOR ADOLESCENTS IN CONFLICT WITH THE LAW 2010.** Available at: <http://www.viablog.org.br/conteudo/LEVANTAMENTO_Socioed.pdf>. Accessed on: 9 July 2011. Annex

also be inferred from the mapping of the growth rates of restriction and deprivation of liberty that, between 2009 and 2010, in the northern region of the country, there was a considerable reduction, in general, in the application of socio-educational measures of internment, provisional internment and semi-liberty. With the exception of the states of Pará and Tocantins, there was a slight increase in the period analysed.

In the Northeast, although some states saw their rates fall, such as Paraíba, Pernambuco, Piauí and Rio Grande do Norte, the others saw an increase in the rate of application of closed measures, with Bahia standing out, where the rate of application of restrictive measures of liberty rose by more than fifty per cent. The same happened in the Centre-West region, where the Federal District recorded an increase of twenty-five per cent, while the other states showed a reduction.

The southern region showed improvements in terms of reducing its rates. However, the state of Paraná saw a significant increase in the application of socio-educational measures of internment and provisional internment, a figure which, when added to the number of adolescents in semi-liberty, is close to one thousand adolescents deprived of their liberty.

Finally, the Southeast region, which has the largest number of adolescents deprived of their liberty, approximately 9,200 inmates, showed a significant increase in its rates, especially in the state of Rio de Janeiro, where the rate of adolescents deprived of their liberty grew by more than 30 per cent. In a different situation is Minas Gerais, where the rate fell by more than eight per cent.

It is important to remember that this data only refers to adolescents deprived of their liberty, which means that it does not show the real situation of violence against children and young people in each region, but only shows the rates of repression of offences considered to be of a serious nature, since socio-educational measures involving deprivation of liberty are an extreme modality, as will be studied in due course. Thus, the situations referred to do not directly reflect the rate of violence, since many of the offences committed may not be compatible with the application of a socio-educational measure in a closed environment and would therefore not be included in this data.

According to official data from the Special Secretariat for Human Rights of the Federative Republic of Brazil and the United Nations Latin American Institute for the Prevention of Crime and the Treatment of Offenders[10], more than half of the offences[11] committed by children and adolescents are property-related, with theft accounting for more than a third of offences committed, followed by illicit drug trafficking, which accounts for around ten per cent.

II.

[10] UNITED NATIONS LATIN AMERICAN INSTITUTE FOR THE PREVENTION OF CRIME AND TREATMENT OF OFFENDERS. **National mapping of open-ended socio-educational measures:** summary report. December 2007. Available at: <http://www.ilanud.org.br/midia/doc/relatorio_resumido_mapeamento_mse_abr2009.pdf>. Accessed on: 09 July 2011. Annex I.

[11] Terminology used when a teenager commits a criminal offence or misdemeanour, according to article 103 of Law 8069/90 - Statute of the Child and Adolescent.

Given this data, the proposal is to study child and adolescent crime and reflect on the model adopted for the treatment of adolescent offenders, analysing existing proposals for legislative changes and their effectiveness. However, a brief historical review of the subject is necessary.

1.2 History of Children's Legislation in Brazil

The question of the history of violence against children and young people in Brazil has been dealt with in different ways over time, leading to the current phase of comprehensive protection, regulated by the Statute of the Child and Adolescent (ECA)[12] . A brief historical contextualisation will help us understand the subject better.

From its discovery until shortly before its independence, Brazil followed Portuguese legislation, at which time there was no explicit concern about the situation of children and adolescents. Naul Luiz Felca teaches[13] that:

> In the Colonial period (1500-1822), international normative acts were used in the national territory, embodied in the Bula Intercoetera (1493, by Pope Alexander VI, which guaranteed the King of Spain rights over America) and the Treaty of Tordesillas (1494), as well as the Ordinances of the Kingdom (Afonsinas, from 1446 to 1521; Manuelinas from 1521 to 1603 and the Philippines, from 1603 to 1830 [...] There was no concern with provisions alluding to children and young people.

When Brazil gained independence in 1822, although the link with the metropolis was extinguished, Roberto Barbosa Alves[14] teaches that there was no immediate break with Lusitanian legislation; on the contrary, the Philippine Ordinances were kept in force in the new Empire, by decree of 20 October 1823.

Later, in 1824, the first Brazilian Constitution was granted, in which there was no reference to children and adolescents. In 1830, the Criminal Code of the Empire regulated the matter, establishing different treatment for young people:

> This piece of legislation provided for the application of correctional measures to minors under the age of 14 who had discernibly committed an anti-social act. From the age of 14 to 17, offenders were punished with a sentence

[12] Law no. 8.069, of 13 July 1990.

[13] FELCA, Naul Luiz. **The 1988 Constitution: a** watershed for children and young people. In: MARTINS, Ives Granda; REZEK, Francisco (Coord.). **Constituição federal: avanços, contribuições e modificações no processo democrático brasileiro.** São Paulo: Ed. Revista dos Tribunais: Centro de Extensão Universitária, 2008. p. 819-820.

[14] ALVES, Roberto Barbosa. **Childhood and youth law.** São Paulo: ed. Saraiva, 2005. p. 2.

corresponding to that of complicity, and from the age of 17 to 21, the penalty was reduced. Imputability began at the age of 21.[15]

The Penal Code of 1890, as Roberto Barbosa Alves teaches[16], provided for non-punishment up to the age of nine, although there was the possibility that young people between the ages of nine and fourteen, when the act was carried out with due discernment, could be sent to a common criminal establishment. The text stipulated that they should be taken to industrial establishments, which did not exist at the time. From the age of fourteen to seventeen, there was a presumption of discernment of the acts carried out by the offender, and from seventeen to twenty-one, age was used as a mitigating factor in the event of a conviction.

In the interregnum between the Penal Code of 1890 and the granting of the Political Charter of 1937, a debate began about the creation of a code that would regulate criminal law for children and adolescents. At the time, the concern was with issues relating to abandonment, deprivation and the practice of so-called anti-social acts by young people.

In this respect, Roberto Barbosa Alves[17] describes that it was at the beginning of the Republic that Senator Lopes Trovão sent the Federal Senate the first bill aimed at special legislation for children and adolescents. Subsequently, other proposals were raised by senators and deputies, with the highlight being the work of magistrate José Cândido de Albuquerque Mello de Mattos, who drafted art. 3° of Law No. 4.242, of 5 January 1921, authorising the government to organise assistance and protection services for abandoned and delinquent young people, as well as providing for the creation of a juvenile court.

Then came the so-called Minors' Code, also known as the Mello de Mattos Code, issued by Decree 17.493-A of 12 October 1927. It created special protection for minors between the ages of fourteen and eighteen, who were classified as abandoned (art. 26), vagrants (art. 28), beggars (art. 29), libertines (art. 30) and delinquents (art. 68 et seq.), as well as establishing that minors under the age of fourteen should remain under the care of their parents.

The Minors' Code remained in force for years in the country's legal system and with the granting of the fourth Federal Constitution, on 10 November 1937, under Getúlio Vargas, the issue was tackled in a pioneering way. Naul Luiz Felca[18] teaches that this was the moment when the state recognised its role in protecting the interests of children and adolescents, and that it should provide

[15] Ibid., p. 3.
[16] Ibid., p. 3-4.
[17] ALVES, Roberto Barbosa. **Childhood and youth law.** São Paulo: ed. Saraiva, 2005. p. 4.
[18] FELCA, Naul Luiz. **The 1988 Constitution: a** watershed for children and young people. In: MARTINS, Ives Granda; REZEK, Francisco (Coord.). **Constituição federal: avanços, contribuições e modificações no processo democrático brasileiro.** São Paulo: Ed. Revista dos Tribunais: Centro de Extensão Universitária, 2008. p. 820-821.

measures to ensure their full physical and moral development in dignified conditions through public policies.

The advent of the 1940 Penal Code, Decree-Law No. 2,848 of 7 December that year, was followed by a great deal of discussion about children and adolescents, an issue of interest both domestically and internationally.

After this innovation, the Constitutions that followed, of 1946, 1967 and 1969, focused on the matter in a succinct way, regulating specific issues such as: prohibitions on certain types of work, maternity assistance, among others, while neglecting issues relating to illegal acts committed by young people.

The discussions that took place were decisive for the changes made to the Minors' Code by Decree Law no. 6.026 of 24 November 1943 and Law no. 5.258 of 10 April 1967.[19] It is important to note that in 1964, through Law no. 4.513, the National Foundation for the Welfare of Minors (FUNABEM) was created, extinguishing the former Service for Assistance to Minors (SAM) and, from then on, each member state of the Federation set up its own unit of the State Foundation for the Welfare of Minors (FEBEM), an establishment for minors to comply with custodial measures, which was eventually replaced by the Foundation for Socio-Educational Care for Adolescents (CASA), in accordance with the guidelines established in the Statute of the Child and Adolescent and the National System for Socio-Educational Care (SINASE).

The Military Penal Code, Decree-Law no. 1001 of 21 October 1969 and the 1969 Penal Code, Decree-Law no. 1004 of 21 October 1969, in their arts. 50 and 33, respectively, provided for the issue of reduced incapacity, i.e. a minor under the age of eighteen would be incapacitated unless, having already reached the age of sixteen, they showed sufficient mental development to understand the illicit nature of the fact and determine themselves accordingly, in which case the applicable penalty would be reduced by one third to one half. However, with the advent of Law n. 6.016, of 31 December 1973, the age of criminal majority was re-established at eighteen (art. 33).

With the various changes to the legislation in force, new guidelines were approved for the Minors' Code, Law 6697 of 10 October 1979, making "an inhumane, brutal and unjust accommodation: it equated abandoned, victimised minors in situations of omission or social risk with perpetrators of offences, calling them minors in an irregular situation (art. 2)."[20] The juvenile judge was also given wide discretion, taking into account the economic and social situation of the minor

---

[19]Both pieces of legislation provide for the measures applicable to minors under the age of 18 for committing acts considered to be criminal offences and make other provisions.

[20] FELCA, Naul Luiz. **The 1988 Constitution: a** watershed for children and young people. In: MARTINS, Ives Granda; REZEK, Francisco (Coord.). **Constituição federal: avanços, contribuições e modificações no processo democrático brasileiro.** São Paulo: Ed. Revista dos Tribunais: Centro de Extensão Universitária, 2008. p. 830.

when making his decision.

Roberto Barbosa Alves[21] criticises the model adopted by the old Juvenile Code, which gave the magistrate broad decision-making powers, and often the judgement was based on the socio-economic and cultural issues of the young person present, and could be applied from a simple warning to internment. It should also be noted that socio-educational proceedings could be initiated by means of an administrative or adversarial procedure, and could be promoted by the Public Prosecutor's Office or anyone who had a legitimate interest in doing so (art. 86).

In the paradigm of the Minors' Code, protection was created for the so-called minor in an irregular situation, classified by Paulo Lúcio Nogueira[22] , as an abandoned minor, i.e. the one who wanders the streets without a family, and the offender, the individual who is the natural consequence of the first figure. However, the latter is dedicated to practising anti-social activities.

João Batista Costa Saraiva states in relation to this Code that "[...] the criminalisation of poverty, the judicialisation of the social question in the orbit of the then Juvenile Law, was what guided the Juvenile Courts of the time."[23]

With the end of the dictatorship, the Federal Constitution was promulgated on 5 October 1988. Also known as the Citizen Constitution, it innovated by creating Chapter VII, Family, Children, Adolescents, Young People and the Elderly, within Title VIII, Social Order.

Article 228 of the Magna Carta establishes the criminal incompetence of minors under the age of eighteen, defining that "minors under the age of eighteen are criminally incompetent, subject to the rules of special legislation." This provision is in line with international movements at the time, which argued that minors under the age of eighteen needed differentiated treatment in view of their civic and psychological training.

This conception is based on the various world conventions that have been promulgated, thus showing the global concern that existed with the issue. Three international documents with the greatest repercussions stand out, which were the pillars of the construction of the Statute of the Child and Adolescent: the Minimum Rules for the Administration of Juvenile Justice, the Guidelines for the Prevention of Juvenile Delinquency (Riyadh Guidelines) and the International Convention on the Rights of the Child.[24]

The Standard Minimum Rules for the Administration of Juvenile Justice, also known as the Beijjing Rules, recommends that "in legal systems that recognise the concept of criminal

---

[21] ALVES, Roberto Barbosa. **Childhood and youth law.** São Paulo: ed. Saraiva, 2005. p. 6-7.

[22] NOGUEIRA, Paulo Lúcio. **Comentários ao código de menores.** 3. ed. São Paulo: Saraiva, 1987. p. XTTT, 9.

[23] SARAIVA, João Batista Costa. **Compendium of juvenile criminal law:** adolescents and offences. 3. ed., rev. and ampl. Porto Alegra: Livraria do Advogado, 2006. p. 26.

[24] Adopted by the United Nations General Assembly under resolutions 40/33, 45/112 and 44/25, respectively.

responsibility for juveniles, its commencement should not be fixed at an excessively early age, taking into account the circumstances that accompany emotional, mental and intellectual maturity" (art. 4.1.)[25] . The Conference also provided for "[...] the protection of juveniles deprived of their liberty in a manner compatible with human rights and fundamental freedoms."[26]

The Guidelines for the Prevention of Juvenile Delinquency[27] , also known as the Riyadh Guidelines, set out some fundamental principles. Among them, art. I° states that the prevention of juvenile delinquency is essential for reducing the number of crimes committed against society, and that young people should be orientated towards useful and socially licit activities, so that they develop good attitudes that are not reprehensible. Referring to the fundamental principles, art. 5° states that community-based services and programmes must be developed to prevent delinquency among children and young people.

The International Convention on the Rights of the Child, in turn, addressed the issue of creating universal rights and guarantees for young people, with the great challenge "[...] being to define universal rights for children, taking into account the diversity of religious, socio-economic and cultural perceptions of childhood in different nations."[28]

Based on these normative instruments, as well as the treatment regulated by the Federal Constitution, Law 8.069, the Statute of the Child and Adolescent (ECA), was published on 13 July 1990, responsible for changing the paradigm from minors in an irregular situation to the full protection of children and adolescents.

1.3 Statute of the Child and Adolescent and the investigation of offences

With the advent of Law 8.069/90, the Statute of the Child and Adolescent (ECA), a new paradigm was created, regulating the special treatment guaranteed to children and adolescents by the Federal Constitution in art. 228[29] . It adopts the so-called doctrine of integral protection[30] (art. 227 of the Federal Constitution).

---

[25] UNICEF. **United Nations Standard Minimum Rules for the Administration of Juvenile Justice (Beijjing Rules).** Available at:
< http://www.dhnet.org.br/direitos/sip/onu/c_a/lex47.htm>. Accessed on: 31 August 2011.

[26] Karina Baptista Sposato. Juvenile Criminal Law, p. 948. apud. PEREIRA, Tânia da Silva. **Direito da criança e do adolescente:** uma proposta interdisciplinar. 2. ed. rev. e atual. Rio de Janeiro: Renovar, 2008. p. 988.

[27] UNICEF. **United Nations Guidelines for the Prevention of Juvenile Delinquency.** Available at: <http://www.mp.rs.gov.br/infancia/documentos_intemacionais/idl03.htm>. Accessed on: 23 August 2011.

[28] PEREIRA, op. cit., p. 952.

[29] Minors under the age of eighteen are criminally incompetent and subject to the rules of special legislation.

[30] This consists of establishing as a duty of the family, society and the state, the integral protection of children and adolescents, with absolute priority, the right to life, health, food, education, leisure, vocational training, culture, dignity, respect, freedom and family and community life, as well as placing them safe from any form of neglect, discrimination, exploitation, violence, cruelty and oppression.

Thus, there is a break with the model of the doctrine of the irregular situation of children and adolescents, regulated in the revoked Minors' Code. To this end, Munir Cury[31] teaches that children and adolescents' rights must be universally recognised, as they protect a section of society that deserves differentiated treatment because they are in full development, and it is the state's role to guarantee the effectiveness and efficacy of measures aimed at all young people under the age of eighteen.

The Statute creates its own legislation for children, who are considered to be those under twelve years of age, and adolescents, who, according to the Statute, are people over twelve and under eighteen years of age.

With regard to criminal offences committed by children or adolescents, the ECA uses the expression "infraction", which consists of the practice of conduct typified in criminal law as a crime or misdemeanour by minors under the age of eighteen.

Thus, children and adolescents who commit an offence will not go unpunished and will be subject to their own so-called socio-educational action. If they are found responsible, some of the measures laid down in the ECA will be applied to them.

In the case of children who have committed an offence, they will be given a protective measure, while adolescents, in the same circumstances, will be given one of the socio-educational measures, with or without a protective measure, at the end of the procedure that investigates the materiality and authorship of the offence and concludes that the claim is well-founded.

These measures, whether protective or socio-educational, are provided for in the ECA and in order to be enforced they require that the child or adolescent be subjected to a socio-educational action before the Children and Youth Court, ensuring all the rights provided for in the Statute, as well as the other rights guaranteed to all people who are subjected to ordinary criminal proceedings.

This is due to the express provision in the Federal Constitution, Article 227 of which establishes that minors under the age of eighteen are considered to be incompetent and will be subject to their own special legislation, in this case the Statute of the Child and Adolescent.

The procedure for this action is regulated in the ECA, starting with art. 171, establishing a special procedural rite, which safeguards the guarantees laid down in the Federal Constitution and the Code of Criminal Procedure, such as due process of law, broad defence, adversarial proceedings, speed, among others.

According to the regulations adopted in the ECA, an adolescent who commits an offence and is caught red-handed[32] must be referred to the police. If the offence has been committed with

---

[31] João Gilberto Lucas Coelho. Criança e Adolescente: a Convenção da ONU e a constituição brasileira, UNICEF, p. 3. apud. CURY, Munir. **Estatuto da criança e do adolescente comentado.** 10. ed. Malheiros. 2010. p. 17-18.

[32] The flagrancy of an offence is based on the rules set out in Article 302 of the Code of Criminal Procedure;

violence or a serious threat to the person, the police authority must draw up an apprehension report, listening to witnesses and the teenager himself. They must also seize the product and instruments of the offence, as well as request the necessary examinations or expertise to prove materiality and authorship.

For João Batista Costa Saraiva "[...] the idea contained in the text translates immediacy, as Paulo Afonso Garrido teaches, according to which, once apprehended, the adolescent must immediately be presented to the competent Police Authority [...]".[33]

In cases where the offence has not been committed by violence or serious threat to the person, the police report may be replaced by a police report, and the adolescent will be released by the police authority upon the appearance of the parents or guardians and the signing of a term of commitment and responsibility to present the adolescent to the Public Prosecutor's Office on the same day, or if this is impossible, on the following day.

If the offence is serious or has major social repercussions, the adolescent may remain in custody as a way of guaranteeing their personal safety or maintaining public order. In this case, the adolescent will be sent by the police authority to the Public Prosecutor's Office, along with a copy of the apprehension report or police report.

If it is impossible for the adolescent to be presented immediately, the police authority will send the adolescent to a care centre, which will present him to the representative of the *Parquet* within 24 hours. If the local authority does not have such a centre, the adolescent will be presented by the police authority itself, and must be sent to a specialised police office. If there is no specialised police office, the adolescent must be kept by the police authority, and under no circumstances may he remain with anyone over the age of eighteen, and must be presented to the representative of the Public Prosecutor's Office within twenty-four hours.

In the event that the adolescent is released and, if there is no evidence of flagrante delicto, there are indications that the adolescent is involved in an offence, the police authority will immediately send a copy of the apprehension report or police report to the Public Prosecutor's Office.

It should be noted that in the case of an offence committed in co-authorship with an adult, they will be brought before the specialised police department and, after the necessary steps have been taken, the adult will be sent to the appropriate police department.

The adolescent may not be driven or transported in a closed compartment of a police vehicle or in conditions that pose a risk to their physical or mental integrity.

Once the adolescent has been presented to the representative of the Public Prosecutor's Office, his informal hearing will be held, as well as that of his parents or legal representatives. In

---

[33] SARAIVA, João Batista Costa. **Compendium of juvenile criminal law:** adolescents and offences. 3. rev. and extended edition. Porto Alegre: Livraria do Advogado, 2006. p. 202.

order to carry out this act, it is possible to use the police.

The Public Prosecutor's Office may then file the case, grant a remission or refer the case to the judicial authority for the application of socio-educational measures.

In the event of a case being dismissed or a remission being granted, the member of the Public Prosecutor's Office must do so in a reasoned manner, presenting a summary of the facts and forwarding it to the Judge for Children and Youth, who must approve the request for dismissal or the granting of remission.

If the judge disagrees with the arguments put forward by the public prosecutor, art. 28 of the Code of Criminal Procedure will apply analogously, and the case file will be forwarded to the Attorney General, who will issue a reasoned order offering representation, appointing another member of the Public *Prosecutor*'s Office to present it, or ratifying the request for closure or remission, in which case the request must be ratified by the judicial authority.

If there is no proposal to shelve or remit the case, the public prosecutor must make a representation to the judicial authority, proposing that proceedings be initiated to investigate the commission of an offence, with a view to holding the offender responsible, with the application of a socio-educational measure.

The representation will contain a brief summary of the facts, the classification of the offence and, where necessary, a list of witnesses, and can be made orally in a daily session organised by the judicial authority. It should be noted, however, that the representation is independent of pre-constituted proof of authorship and materiality.

A request for provisional detention can be made cumulatively with the offer of representation, and the member of the *Public Prosecutor*'s Office can also request that it be revoked if it has been decreed previously.

Once the representation has been made, the judicial authority will set a date for a hearing to be held, deciding from the outset whether to order or maintain provisional detention, and the adolescent and their parents or guardians will be informed of the content of the representation and notified to attend the designated hearing, accompanied by a lawyer.

In the event of a hypothesis in which the provisional detention of an adolescent is appropriate, this will be along the lines of precautionary detention, in accordance with the provisions of article 312 of the Code of Criminal Procedure. However, it is an exceptional measure and has some peculiarities covered by the ECA:

> Incidentally, as a fundamental right of citizenship, the deprivation of liberty of adolescents will only be permitted when they are caught in the act of committing a criminal offence or by a written and reasoned order from the judicial authority, and it has already been established that the maximum

> period for which adolescents can be provisionally interned cannot exceed 45 days, a guarantee guaranteed in two provisions of the Statute (arts. 108 and 183).[34]

If the parents cannot be found, a special curator will be appointed for the teenager. If the adolescent is not found, the judicial authority will issue a search and seizure warrant, ordering the case to be suspended until he or she is actually presented. If the teenager is in hospital, they will be requested to appear, without prejudice to notifying their parents or guardian.

At the presentation hearing, the adolescent and his or her parents or guardian will be heard. If the authority considers that a remission is appropriate, it will hear the representative of the Public Prosecutor's Office and then issue its decision.

In the case of a serious offence, subject to socio-educational measures of internment or semi-liberty, and if the adolescent does not have a lawyer, the judge will appoint a lawyer and set a date for a continuation hearing, and the adolescent must present a preliminary defence and a witness list within three days of the presentation hearing.

At the continuation hearing, after the witnesses listed in the representation and in the prior defence have been heard, the steps have been taken and the report from the interprofessional team has been attached, the member of the Public Prosecutor's Office and the Defender will be given twenty minutes in turn, after which the judge will hand down a decision.

It is important to note that the judge will not apply any of the measures if, when passing sentence, he or she recognises that the fact does not exist, or that there is no proof of its existence, or that it does not constitute an offence, or that there is no proof that the adolescent contributed to the offence.

If the representation is upheld, in the case of the application of a socio-educational measure of internment or semi-liberty, the summons must be served on the adolescent, who will express their desire to appeal the sentence or not, as well as their defender. If the adolescent cannot be found, the summons may be served on their parents or legal guardian and, in the case of any other socio-educational measure applied, the summons will be served on their defence counsel.

Finally, it is worth noting that the maximum time limit for concluding the procedure is forty-five days in the case of a provisionally interned adolescent. It should also be noted that the detention cannot be carried out in a prison and, in the event that the district does not have a suitable facility, the adolescent must be transferred to the nearest district and, if transfer is impossible, the adolescent must be removed to a police station, in an isolated section for adults, for a maximum of five days.

---

[34] SARAIVA, João Batista Costa. **Compendium of juvenile criminal law:** adolescents and offences. 3. ed., rev. and amp. Porto Alegre: Livraria do Advogado, 2006. p. 96-97.

1.4 Socio-educational measures regulated by the Statute of the Child

Children and adolescents who commit offences are subject to socio-educational action in order to be held accountable for their actions. If the offender is a teenager and the materiality and authorship of the offence have been proven, at the end of the proceedings one of the measures laid down in the ECA will be applied.

Despite disagreements about the legal nature of these measures, it is certain that they have a re-socialising purpose, and that it is essential to develop educational and social activities when children or adolescents comply with them.

For Wilson Donizete Liberati, the socio-educational measure is:

> [...] it is equivalent to a penalty, the meaning of which implies a sanction applied as punishment or reparation for an offence judged to be reprehensible. Its execution, however, must be a pedagogical instrument, aimed at adjusting the offender's behaviour to peaceful social coexistence, under the prism of special prevention, aimed at the future.[35]

He also states that socio-educational measures "like any restriction of freedom imposed coercively as a consequence of the violation of a rule, are punishments or sanctions. Not recognising this character increases the sense of mystification and manipulation experienced by the offenders themselves."[36]

A similar view is held by Karina Baptista Sposato[37] , who believes that socio-educational measures are criminal in nature, i.e. the adolescent is held responsible through a socio-educational action and the state can apply a measure that infringes on their freedom of movement or involves doing something. Thus, although it has pedagogical aspects, the structure it is moulded on is similar to that of penalties.

The model adopted by the ECA with regard to offences and socio-educational measures is one of the most advanced in the world and is in line with international treaties to which Brazil is a signatory, with reference to the full protection of children and adolescents, who are at a stage of development.

For the application of socio-educational measures, the adolescent in conflict with the law will be subjected to a socio-educational action, with the judge ultimately deciding on one or more protection measures, as well as, if appropriate, one of the socio-educational measures. The same

---

[35] Wilson Donizete Liberati. Juvenile criminal procedure. São Paulo: Malheiros, 2006. p. 145. apud. PEREIRA, Tânia da Silva. **Direito da criança e do adolescente:** uma proposta interdisciplinar. 2. ed. rev. e atual. Rio de Janeiro: Renovar. 2008. p. 988.

[36] ALVES, Roberto Barbosa. **Childhood and youth law.** São Paulo: Saraiva, 2005. p. 90.

[37] PEREIRA, op. cit., p. 114.

applies to children, but only protective measures can be applied to them.

Of course, the process to which they will be subjected differs from the model defined in the Code of Criminal Procedure. However, the latter may be applied on a subsidiary basis, in accordance with the provisions of Article 152 of the ECA.

Protection measures are included in articles 98 et seq. of the ECA, and are generally aimed at guaranteeing the minimum rights of children and adolescents, such as: health, education, medical and psychological treatment, inclusion in community programmes, placement in a substitute family, among others.

These will be applied when the child or adolescent's rights are threatened or violated by action or omission on the part of society or the state; by fault, omission or abuse on the part of the parents or guardian; or, due to their conduct, if the latter is involved in criminal offences. Its application can be isolated or cumulative with others, and can be changed at any time.

Examples include referral to parents or guardians, by means of a statement of responsibility; guidance, support and temporary accompaniment; compulsory enrolment and attendance at an official primary school; institutional foster care, placement in a substitute family, among others.

It is important to emphasise that protective measures will usually be granted through socio-educational action, however, in some cases provided for in the ECA, the Guardianship Council and the Public Prosecutor's Office may act *ex officio* .[38]

Socio-educational measures are applied in accordance with the seriousness of the offence committed, the circumstances in which it took place and the subjective characteristics of the offender (art. 112, ECA).

Thus, if the offender is a primary offender and the offence is not considered serious, in theory a more lenient socio-educational measure will be applied; in the opposite situation, a more serious measure.

Socio-educational measures are provided for in the ECA, starting with Article 112, and their list is exhaustive. They are: a warning, an obligation to repair the damage, community service, probation, semi-liberty and internment.

As already mentioned, these measures do not have the character of a sanction, but rather a re-socialising function, to reintegrate the child or adolescent into society. The measures regulated in the ECA are peculiar because the defendants are people undergoing physical and psychological development and therefore, in accordance with the Political Charter, require special treatment.

The warning measure, provided for in art. 115, consists of a verbal admonishment of the adolescent in conflict with the law, as well as their parents.

---

[38] According to articles 93, 136, inc. I and 201, inc. VIII, all of the ECA.

As Tânia da Silva Pereira explains, the warning "[...] aims to make clear to the adolescent the inappropriateness of his conduct, enabling him to have his offence recognised as such by an authority."[39]

The purpose of this measure is to inform and make the offender aware that his behaviour is frowned upon by society, and it also serves as a warning that if he resumes committing offences, a more severe measure will be imposed.

The socio-educational measure of the obligation to repair the damage caused, set out in Article 116, provides for the possibility of the adolescent repairing the damage caused to the victim, in cases where the offence committed is related to their property.

If the offender is unable to compensate the victim, another measure will be imposed. Wilson Donizete Liberati considers that:

> The purpose of the measure is to make the teenager feel responsible for the act they have committed and to intensify the necessary care so as not to cause harm to others. For this reason, there is an understanding that this measure is very personal and non-transferable, and that the teenager should be solely responsible for repairing the damage.[40]

João Batista Costa Saraiva agrees:

> [...] the important thing is that the adolescent himself is able to repair the damage, and this measure should not be confused with the compensation for the damage made by the adolescent's parents (of a civil liability nature, inherent to the species, a corollary of the exercise of Family Power). The reparation of the damage must be the result of the teenager's actions, by their own means, working with the victim themselves, often in a restorative way. Hence its educational nature.[41]

The community service measure, provided for in Article 117 of the ECA, is a way for adolescents to directly repair the harm caused to society. To this end, they will be assigned tasks in line with their aptitudes.

It's important to note that this service will not interfere with the teenager's school day or work period, and can even be carried out at weekends and on public holidays. What's more, the hours to be worked are eight per week.

---

[39] Wilson Donizete Liberati. Juvenile criminal procedure. São Paulo: Malheiros, 2006. p. 145. apud. PEREIRA, Tânia da Silva. **Direito da criança e do adolescente:** uma proposta interdisciplinar. 2. ed. rev. e atual. Rio de Janeiro: Renovar. 2008. p. 988.

[40] Wilson Donizete Liberati. Adolescents and offences: is a socio-educational measure a crime?, p. 105. apud. PEREIRA, Tânia da Silva. **Direito da criança e do adolescente:** uma proposta interdisciplinar. 2. ed. rev. e atual. Rio de Janeiro: Renovar. 2008. p. 995.

[41] SARAIVA, João Batista Costa. **Compendium of juvenile criminal law:** adolescents and offences. 3. ed., rev. and expanded. Porto Alegre: Livraria do Advogado, 2006. p. 158.

Wilson Donizete Liberati considers that "[...] measures carried out in the community and family context enable young people to re-examine their conduct, assess the consequences and propose a change in behaviour, with the indication that they will no longer participate in illegal acts."[42]

For Roberto Bergalli, the socio-educational measure of community service is linked to the idea of a punitive nature:

> [...] the submission of an adolescent to 'community service' has a highly educational meaning, particularly aimed at forcing the adolescent to become aware of the values involved in social solidarity practised at its most expressive levels. Assisting the disadvantaged, the sick and the educated (activities that must be carried out in "welfare organisations, hospitals, schools and other similar establishments") is a task that requires confrontation with the collective *alter,* so that a reciprocal trust can be demonstrated, which in turn is present in all codes of community ethics, as an inheritance from religious decalogues.[43]

The measure of probation, provided for in articles 118 et seq. of the ECA, is designed to accompany, help and guide adolescent offenders. To this end, the adolescent will be looked after by a team or organisation appointed by the Judge for Children and Youth, which will be responsible for promoting the adolescent socially, supervising school attendance and performance, submitting reports and working towards professionalisation.

For Mário Volpi, the educational function of the measure "[...] manifests itself in personalised monitoring, guaranteeing the following aspects: protection, community integration, daily life, maintaining family ties, school attendance, integration into the labour market and/or vocational and training courses." [44]

The Judge for Children and Youth must set the measure for a minimum period of six months, and it may be replaced or revoked, provided the counsellor, the Public Prosecutor's Office and the Defender are heard.

The semi-liberty measure, provided for in art. 120, consists of a more rigorous measure, since it partially deprives the adolescent of their freedom. This measure can be applied at the end of the process, as well as serving as a transition from the internment measure to one of the open-ended measures.

It is important to note that schooling and professionalisation of the adolescent is compulsory

---

[42] PEREIRA, Tânia da Silva. Direito da criança e do adolescente - uma proposta interdisciplinar. Rio de Janeiro: Renovar, 2008. p. 1001. apud. Wilson Donizete Liberati. **Adolescents and offences: is a socio-educational measure a penalty?,** p. 98-99.

[43] CURY, Munir. **Estatuto da criança e do adolescente comentado.** 7. ed. rev. and updated. São Paulo: Malheiros, 2005. p . 399.

[44] VOLPI, Mário, (org.) O adolescente e o ato infracional, p. 24. Apud. PEREIRA, Tânia da Silva. **Child and adolescent law:** an interdisciplinary proposal. Rio de Janeiro: Renovar, 2008. p. 1001.

during their time in detention, as well as the fact that there is no specific time limit for this, but that it must respect the limits imposed on the internment measure.

With regard to this socio-educational measure, Wilson Donizete Liberati considers that:

> The partial deprivation of liberty of the adolescent offender stems from the objective of the measure under study: its function is to punish the adolescent who has committed an offence. It is true, however, that all socio-educational measures - including semi-freedom - have a sanctioning-punitive nature, with a true symptom of retribution for the act committed, carried out with a pedagogical purpose.[45]

Mauro Ferrandim[46] ponders that "the physical space destined for the programme is characterised by the similarity it should have to a home, because in it the adolescent will have the freedom to express themselves individually, while still imposing limitations [...]."

Finally, as an extreme measure, there is internment, in accordance with the provisions of art.

121 et seq. of the ECA. As in criminal law, this measure should be used as a *last resort.* The guiding principles of this measure stand out, which are: brevity, exceptionality and respect for the condition of the developing person, supported by the Federal Constitution, in art. 227, § 3° , inc. V.

In view of the above, the Statute of the Child and Adolescent explicitly provides for the hypotheses in which it can be applied when the offence is committed by violence or serious threat to the person; for repeated serious offences; or when there is repeated and unjustified non-compliance with a previously applied measure.

It should be noted that, in the latter case, there is the so-called internment-sanction, in which the adolescent will be returned to internment for a maximum period of three months, which must be decreed by the courts after due legal process, in accordance with the provisions of § I° , of art. 122 of the ECA.

The internment measure will be applied for an indefinite period and, while deprived of their liberty, it will be the state's duty to guarantee the interned adolescent access to education, professionalisation, culture, sport, leisure, as well as the other guarantees granted to all people deprived of their liberty. Article 125 of the ECA states that: "It is the duty of the state to ensure the physical and mental integrity of inmates, and it is up to the state to adopt appropriate measures of

---

[45] Wilson Donizete Liberati. Adolescente e Ato Infracional: Medida Socioeducativa é Pena?, p. 116. apud. PEREIRA, Tânia da Silva. **Child and adolescent law:** an interdisciplinary proposal. Rio de Janeiro: Renovar, 2008. p. 1002.

[46] FERRANDIN, Mauro. **Juvenile criminal act** - applicability of the principles and guarantees of the criminal act. Curitiba: Juruá, 2009. p. 83.

containment and security."

On this issue, Tânia da Silva Pereira considers that "[...] the lack of suitable institutions and an effective methodological plan to promote the re-education of adolescent offenders will undoubtedly strip the socio-educational measure of its pedagogical nature, turning it into a punitive measure".[47]

Once again, it should be pointed out that adolescents are considered to be developing people and, because of this, it is important that they are motivated to take part in educational and social activities, since the measure aims to re-socialise them.

This measure is carried out in specific establishments, separate from ordinary prisoners. The term stipulated by the Juvenile Court Judge is indeterminate, and under no circumstances may it exceed three years, as set out in § 3° of art. 121. Once this period has been reached, the adolescent must be released and a measure of semi-liberty or probation imposed.

Adolescents who are serving a socio-educational detention order and reach the age of eighteen will remain in custody until they reach twenty-one, unless they are released earlier.

During the sentence, studies will be carried out every six months on the performance of the interned adolescent, addressed to the Judge of the Court and the Children's Court, who will assess whether they are fit to return to social life and, in this way, the measure imposed may be upgraded to an open-ended one. If he or she does not demonstrate that he or she is capable of returning to social life, he or she must be kept in detention by means of a reasoned decision.

It is also important to note that in any case of disintimation, this will be preceded by judicial authorisation, and the Public Prosecutor's Office must be heard, according to § 6° of art. 121.

[47] Wilson Donizete Liberati. Adolescente e Ato Infracional: Medida Socioeducativa é Pena?, p. 116. apud. PEREIRA, Tânia da Silva. **Child and adolescent law:** an interdisciplinary proposal. Rio de Janeiro: Renovar, 2008. p. 1005.

CHAPTER 2

AGE OF CRIMINAL RESPONSIBILITY, CRITERIA FOR SETTING IT AND COMPARATIVE LAW

2.1 Age as a coefficient of Penal Majority

As shown in the previous chapter, the Brazilian legislature has dealt with the issue of the starting point for criminal responsibility in different ways over the years. However, in the face of international pressure to set a reasonable age for holding young people responsible for committing illicit acts, it was necessary to separate the imputable from the imputable, in response to social concerns.

Even though child and adolescent violence has increased significantly over the years, according to the data already presented, the Statute of the Child and Adolescent ensures that offenders under the age of eighteen are treated differently. However, when serious criminal acts are committed that mobilise the whole country, the question arises as to the special treatment given to young people, and the possibility of changing the legislation so that they are criminally liable for their actions.

In situations of social commotion, the media, especially the sensationalist media, take the opportunity to explore the problem as if it were an isolated event in which only young people were responsible for the violence, failing to analyse crime as a whole, as well as the reasons that cause its rise, such as unemployment, social inequality, problems with education and health, among others.

Despite the importance of society's discussion in the quest to improve Brazil's legislation for children and adolescents, which is a benchmark for several Latin American countries, the discourse presented does not seem capable of creating an approach aimed at reducing violence, but merely seeks a way to punish those who commit illegal acts.

The entire doctrinal construction of the integral protection of children and adolescents, a milestone in the political-ideological transition from the Code of Minors to the Statute of the Child and Adolescent, is destroyed by these inconsequential speeches, which are often nothing more than fallacies, presented in moments of popular commotion, giving rise to movements clamouring for changes in legislation for children and adolescents, demanding a reduction in the age of criminal responsibility.

The Federal Constitution, in art. 228, and the ECA, in art. 104, define that "minors under the age of eighteen are criminally incompetent", a determination in line with the International Convention on the Rights of the Child, issued by the United Nations (UN) in 1989, which, in its preamble, recognises that children and adolescents need special treatment, since they are in full physical and intellectual-volitional development.

Regarding the age limit adopted by Brazil, João Batista Saraiva teaches[48] that the age established as the starting point for the age of criminal majority was not randomly set by the Brazilian legislature. On the contrary, discussions were held in international forums in which various countries presented their points of view on the subject, with Brazil opting to implement the model of full protection for children and adolescents when it enacted the Statute of the Child and Adolescent to replace the old model of the minor in an irregular situation, adopted by the Minors' Code.

The ECA adopted the biological criterion for defining the age of criminal responsibility, considering anyone under the age of eighteen to be incompetent. On reaching that age, the young person is no longer protected by special legislation and is now criminally liable for their actions. This does not mean that minors under the age of eighteen will go unpunished for any offences committed. They will be subjected to socio-educational proceedings, in which one of the socio-educational measures may be applied, which may even be restrictive of liberty.

Thus, although there are criticisms of the criteria used by the legislator when setting the initial age of criminal majority, it must be recognised that there has been a great deal of academic and social discussion about its delimitation. Furthermore, it is an incontrovertible fact that a number of innovations have taken place in all fields of human knowledge since its stipulation and, as a result, there has been discussion about new perspectives on legislation for children and adolescents, since these changes have created changes in the factual context of today's society, to which the rules laid down in the Statute of the Child and Adolescent and the Federal Constitution are opposed.

In this context, the current stage of cultural and technological development means that young people have access to a lot of information much more quickly and efficiently than they did in the early 90s. Thus, regardless of the change in the age of majority, it is necessary to readjust the statutory rules.

At the present time, it is safe to say that a child of twelve or thirteen has sufficient discernment to know that stealing someone else's property or killing another person, for example, are considered criminal acts disapproved of by society.

This knowledge of right and wrong, good and evil, is passed on to children and adolescents during the process of education, which begins in their early years at home. Later, when children and teenagers are already attending school and thus taking part in activities together with other people in their age group, all the learning is put into practice and, from then on, the formation of their character and posture can be analysed.

This demonstrates the importance of the educational process, whether at home with parents

---

[48] SARAIVA, João Batista Costa. **Compendium of juvenile criminal law:** adolescents and offences. 3. ed. rev. and expanded. Porto Alegre: Livraria do Advogado, 2006. p. 33.

or at school, because it is during this period that young people add values that they will carry with them for life, thus establishing the pillars that will be decisive in their future choices, reflecting directly on the attitudes they take and, above all, in the formation of their character and values.

This is not to say that the age of criminal responsibility should be reduced, nor that it should be maintained. What we are trying to do is demonstrate the importance that must be given to revising statutory provisions in the face of technological and social advances.

2.2 The criteria used to establish the starting point for criminal liability

In accordance with international treaties, the Federal Constitution in force guarantees differentiated treatment for children and adolescents, and regulates this treatment through the ECA. Using the biopsychological criterion and aiming for accountability when committing offences, a person over the age of eighteen who does not have any mental pathology is defined as imputable, and is held criminally responsible for committing a crime or misdemeanour, whether their conduct is intentional or culpable. In relation to children and adolescents who commit offences, the biological criterion will be used, so the simple fact that they are eighteen years old at the time of the offence is enough for them to be protected by statutory legislation and, given the rules established therein, be held responsible for the offence committed.

Thus, the starting point for criminal responsibility is set at the age of eighteen, as a criminal policy option that takes into account aspects relating to biological, cognitive and intellectual development, factors that are decisive in shaping an individual's character.

Carlos Eduardo Barreiros Rebelo[49] teaches that, "[...] each society has the autonomy to define what is considered a child and what is considered an adolescent. These definitions are based on historical and social criteria."

With regard to the psychological maturation of young people, Flávio Augusto Monteiro de Barros[50] highlights two important moments in human development: the intellective stage, which occurs when the child or adolescent is able to discern between right and wrong. At this stage, it is not important to know what is or is not permitted by law, but it is only necessary for them to know whether or not the act has caused any harmful effects for others; the second moment, called volitional, is when the will must be externalised in accordance with the law, in other words, the conduct is carried out with sufficient discernment to know whether or not it is in accordance with the legal system.

Regarding the importance given to discernment of the conduct committed, in other words,

---

[49] REBELO, Carlos Eduardo Barreiros. **The age of criminal majority and the controversy over its reduction.** Belo Horizonte: Jus, 2010. p. 41-42.

[50] BARROS, Flávio Augusto Monteiro de. **Criminal law:** general part. 7. ed. São Paulo: Saraiva, 2009. p. 386.

whether or not the young person had full knowledge of the repercussions of their actions, Jesús-Maria Silva Sánchez teaches[51] that:

> *"The model of judgement, which has its origins in Roman Law, and which, through Canon Law, influences both the systems of continental European codification and those of Comon Law, has very specific theoretical foundations and, at the same time, is based on practical assumptions that must be highlighted. As far as the theoretical foundations of the system are concerned, it is based on a retributive conception of punishment: it is therefore conceived as a punishment that restores the justice violated by the commission of the offence. It also starts from the idea that guilt, understood as a judgement of reproach, is an essential prerequisite for punishment, through the so-called bilateral concept of guilt. According to this, if there is no guilt, the penalty cannot be imposed, but vice versa, whenever there is guilt, a penalty must be imposed. "*[52]

In line with what Silva Sánchez says, Carlos Eduardo Barreiros Rebelo[53] believes that most children and adolescents don't have the capacity to understand the harm that can come from criminal behaviour. They are people in full development and therefore deserve different treatment from adults. He also argues that the maturation process takes place through the social relationships experienced and established with the outside world, which provides an exchange of views on different realities, an important factor in the formation and development of young people.

It should be noted that although the ECA has adopted the biological criterion when defining the starting point for criminal responsibility, there are other parameters used to understand special protection. Damásio Evangelista de Jesus[54] teaches that the following criteria can be used to determine criminal responsibility: biological, adopted by the legislation for children and adolescents, which establishes that in the absence of any mental pathology or any crises of psychological disorders, a young person under the age of eighteen will be subject to the statutory rules; the psychological criterion, which takes into account the fact that at the time the criminal act was committed, the perpetrator was or was not in a position to discern whether or not their behaviour was contrary to the law; and, finally, the biopsychological criterion, which consists of a combination of the two previous

---

[51] SÁNCHEZ, Jesús-Maria Silva. La política criminal ante el hecho penalmente antijurídico cometido por un menor de edad. In: FRANCO, Alberto Silva; NUCCI, Guilherme de Souza. (**Criminal law.** São Paulo: Revista dos Tribunais, 2010. v. 7. p. 759.

[52] "The discernment model, which has its origins in Roman Law, and which, through Canon Law, influences both the codification system on the European continent and the *Comon Law* system, because it has very concrete theoretical foundations and, at the same time, starts from the practical assumption that they must be emphasised. While the theoretical foundations of the system are based on a retributive conception of punishment: it is therefore granted as a punishment that restores the justice violated by the commission of an offence. It is also based on the idea that guilt, understood as a judgement of disapproval, is an essential prerequisite for punishment, through the so-called bilateral theory of guilt. According to this, if there is no guilt, the penalty cannot be imposed, and vice versa, whenever there is guilt, a penalty must be imposed. - Our translation.

[53] REBELO, Carlos Eduardo Barreiros. **The age of criminal majority and the controversy over its reduction.** Belo Horizonte: Jus, 2010. p. 41-42, 47.

[54]JESUS, Damásio E. de. **Criminal law:** general part. 31. ed. São Paulo: Saraiva, 2010. vol. 1. p. 544.

criteria, adopted by the legislator in the Penal Code with regard to criminal offences committed by those found guilty.

The Statute of the Child and Adolescent, following the constitutional provision, adopted the biological criterion for committing offences. Damásio E. de Jesus[55] teaches that the legislator opted for an absolute presumption of imputability and, thus, "[...] minority (biological factor) is already sufficient to create imputability: the Code absolutely presumes that a person under 18 'is entirely incapable of understanding the illicit nature of the fact' and 'of determining themselves in accordance with that understanding'."

The biological model for measuring the age of criminal majority consists of establishing an age at which it is reasonable to expect that the child or adolescent has acquired sufficient maturity to discern between right and wrong. João Batista Costa Saraiva[56] teaches that:

> Considering intellectual development and average access to information, it's clear that any young person at the age of 16, 14 or 12 is capable of understanding the illegal nature of certain acts. In fact, even small children know that you can't kill, that hurting another person is "ugly" or that you're not allowed to take another person's object for yourself. The old Roman Catechism already considered the age of seven to be the "age of reason", from which it is possible to "commit a mortal sin". This reasoning about discernment, taken to its ultimate consequences, can lead to the conclusion that a child, regardless of their age, should be subjected to criminal proceedings and eventually sent to prison, as long as they are capable of distinguishing "good" from "evil".

Although Brazil has adopted the model of full protection for children and adolescents, as well as the biological criterion for setting the age of criminal majority, it is important to emphasise that, regardless of the position adopted on whether or not to lower the age of criminal responsibility, the historical, economic and socio-cultural moment of the time in which this legislation was passed must be taken into account. The protection of minors under the age of eighteen in current legislation deserves, at the very least, a readjustment to the current social paradigm, which differs completely from that of the late 1980s and early 1990s.

The technological evolution that has taken place over the period from the aforementioned period to the present day, as well as changes in social relations as a whole, have undergone significant changes. The means of communication, whatever they may be, are more diverse, efficient and accessible these days, with any world event being broadcast live and simultaneously to all countries. The same can be said for means of transport, knowledge, culture and so many other areas that have

---

[55] Ibid., p. 550.

[56] SARAIVA, João Batista Costa. **Compendium of juvenile criminal law:** adolescents and offences. 3. ed. revised and updated. Porto Alegre: Livraria do Advogado, 2006. p. 52.

an impact on human life.

The term globalisation, which refers to a change in paradigms, is also present in the legal field. This means that new laws are created and others are revised or adapted to the new economic, historical and political-social realities of a given moment. So it's safe to say that a child or adolescent from the early 1990s is completely different from those of today, including in terms of their values.

Regardless of the position to be adopted on maintaining or lowering the starting age for criminal responsibility, the ECA needs its provisions to be readjusted or updated, because although children and adolescents continue to have this *status* and therefore need special treatment, their values have changed over time.

Despite the points regarding the issue of discernment, the incontrovertible fact is that children and adolescents need special protection because they are in a phase of development and formation of a critical sense. Carlos Eduardo Barreiros Rebelo[57] warns that children under the age of eighteen, given the current system, have a better chance of being reintegrated into society and stop committing offences than adults, who have little chance of changing their character, which has already been duly formed.

Leo Van Holthe, quoting Weber de Moura Agra, states that "[...] this limit on criminal imputability is justified because children and adolescents are still in the process of forming their character, their personality, so that society can prepare them for social interaction [...]." [58]

Renata Franchi Stênico[59] , in her final course work, argues that:

> Childhood and adolescence are considered essential stages of preparation for adulthood, whereas old age is its disintegration. Adolescence therefore ends when a person acquires an identity, i.e. chooses a profession and associates with other people on an equal footing. This is not as exact as a mathematical sum; for some it may happen earlier, for others later.

It is clear that, regardless of the age at which the age of criminal responsibility is set, childhood and adolescence are essential stages in anyone's life. Brazil's choice of age for criminal responsibility has also been determined by the criminal policy adopted by the state.

From this perspective, the Penal Code, in its Explanatory Memorandum of Part General, clarifies that:

[37] REBELO, Carlos Eduardo Barreiros. **The age of criminal majority and the controversy over its reduction.** Belo Horizonte: Jus, 2010. p. 56.

[58] HOLTHE, Leo Van. **Constitutional Law.** 5. ed. rev., ampl. e atual. Salvador: Jus Podivm, 2009. p. 808.

[59] STENCIO, Renata Franchi. The age of majority: a political and legal choice. 2008. 66 f. Final Coursework. (Law degree). Faculty of History, Law and Social Work, Universidade Estadual Paulista "Júlio de Mesquita Filho", Franca, 2008. p. 18-19.

> The Bill maintained the criminal unimputability of children under 18. This option is based on criminal policy criteria. Those who advocate lowering the limit on the grounds of growing crime, which recruits a greater number of minors every day, fail to consider the fact that minors, being still incomplete, are naturally anti-social to the extent that they are not socialised or educated. The readjustment of the process of character formation should be entrusted to education, not criminal punishment. Moreover, with the recently enacted legislation on minors, the state has the necessary instruments to remove young offenders under the age of 18 from social interaction, without their having to undergo the treatment of adult offenders, exposing them to prison contamination.[60]

As a result of a criminal policy that involves various factors, the legislator adopted the age of eighteen as the starting point for criminal responsibility, thereby guaranteeing these individuals the special treatment provided for in the Federal Constitution and regulated by the Statute of the Child and Adolescent.

On the consummation of the age of criminal majority, when the young person ceases to be considered unimputable and becomes imputable under criminal law, Van Holthe teaches[61] that "the jurisprudence and doctrine of the country consider that the individual who commits the crime on the day he turns 18 is imputable, regardless of the time he was born and the exact moment of the crime", and this is the understanding established by the Federal Supreme Court:

> The allegation of minority must be proven, in criminal proceedings, by specific and suitable documentary evidence, consisting of the certificate extracted from the birth certificate of the accused, charged or convicted. Court precedents. The mere invocation by the patient of his condition as a minor, unaccompanied by suitable evidence - the birth certificate - is insufficient to justify acceptance of his claim (HC 68.466/DF, Trib. Pleno, STF, rei. Min. Celso de Mello, j. 19.12.90, DJ 09.03.91, p. 2204).

It should be emphasised that although when the Civil Code was enacted, Law no. 10.406, of 10 January 2002, the legislator established the age of civil majority at eighteen years of age, according to the provisions of art. 5° , this fact does not in any way influence the

age of criminal responsibility, as these are different fields of law with different repercussions. Roberto Barbosa Alves teaches[62] that:

> One of the most eloquent changes introduced by the reform, the reduction of civil capacity from 21 to 18 years of age (art. 5°), could not pass unscathed

[60] Explanatory Memorandum Penal Code General Part.

[61] HOLTHE, Leo Van. **Constitutional Law.** 5 ed. revised, expanded and updated. Salvador: Jus Podivm, 2009. p. 808.

[62] ALVES, Roberto Barbosa. **Childhood and youth law.** São Paulo: Saraiva, 2005. p.62.

in this process. The abolition of the age limit of 21, and the consequent equalisation of the civil liability framework with the criminal liability framework, could seduce some interpreters into thinking that the new Civil Code interferes with the rules for prosecuting offences under the ECA, preventing the application of any measure to a person who, having committed an offence before the age of 18, reaches that age. This means, for example, that anyone who, on the eve of their 18th birthday, set out to eliminate all their enemies would go unpunished.

2.3 The treatment of the age of criminal majority in foreign legal systems

The Brazilian Statute for Children and Adolescents served as the basis for the development of legislation for children and adolescents in Latin America. The Standard Minimum Rules for the Administration of Juvenile Justice, the Guidelines for the Prevention of Juvenile Delinquency (Riyadh Guidelines) and the International Convention on the Rights of the Child were decisive in the dissemination of new legislation around the world.

However, even though there are international criteria on the legislation of children and adolescents, it must be borne in mind that each country is sovereign and therefore not bound to use a pre-established age; on the contrary, this will be determined in accordance with the criminal policy of the country in question, as well as the historical, cultural and socio-economic reality of each state.

As a result, the starting point for criminal responsibility is set at different ages around the world.[63] In order to exemplify the breadth of the discussion, Julio Fabbrini Mirabete[64] points out that each country adopts an age for establishing the age of criminal responsibility, which is set at: seventeen years of age in countries such as Greece, New Zealand, Malaysia; sixteen in Argentina, the Philippines, Belgium and Israel; fifteen in India, Egypt, Paraguay and Lebanon; fourteen in Germany and Haiti; and ten years of age in England. It should be noted, however, that countries such as Denmark, France, Mexico, Cuba and the Netherlands, among others, set the age of criminal majority at eighteen.

Mirabete[65] also points out that some countries have adopted the age of eighteen as the starting point for criminal responsibility, such as Sweden and Chile, which have set the age at twenty-one in the interests of criminal policy.

The aforementioned author[66] also teaches that in the United States of America, in view of

---

[63] See Annex III;

[64] MIRABETE, Júlio Fabbrini. **Manual of criminal law:** general part. 25. ed. rev. and updated. São Paulo: Atlas, 2009. vol. 1. p. 202.

[65] MIRABETE, Júlio Fabbrini. **Manual of criminal law:** general part. 25. ed. rev. and updated. São Paulo: Atlas, 2009. vol. 1. p. 202.

[66] idem.

its colonisation and political and cultural background, each Member State is given the power to legislate and, as a result, the issue is dealt with in a variety of ways. For example, states such as Massachusetts, Michigan, Missouri and Texas set the age of criminal responsibility at seventeen, while New York and North Carolina set the starting point for criminal responsibility at sixteen. Kentucky, on the other hand, set the age of majority at fourteen.

With regard to Asian and European countries, data from UNICEF[67] shows that in Japan, children under the age of twenty will be prosecuted in the Family Court and not in the ordinary Criminal Court. In China, young people between the ages of fourteen and eighteen who commit offences are judged by a special court, but if the offence is judged to be serious, they could be sentenced to life imprisonment, while in Scandinavian countries, criminal responsibility is established at the age of fifteen, and adolescents between the ages of eighteen and fifteen are subject to community service and, in the last resort, deprived of their liberty.

As far as the Scottish model is concerned, Gerry Maher[68] , in an article entitled "Age and Criminal Responsibility", reports that the Scottish system has established the age of criminal majority at eight years of age since 1932, and needs to be changed. To this end, he states that:

> *At first sight this age seems low. However, it might be thought that children are developing at a faster rate than previously. Today children eightyears of age have a greater understanding of the world (certainly of technology) than the seven-year-old children in the eighteenth and nineteenth centwies (when the rule in Scots law developed). This might then suggest that there could be a case for lowering the age in the Scottish rule from eight to a* 69 *younger age.*

Portuguese law establishes the age of criminal majority at sixteen, and the Portuguese Penal Code, Decree-Law no. 400, of 23 September 1982, updated by Law no. 59, of 4 September 2007, establishes in its article 9° , that "rules laid down in special legislation apply to those over sixteen and under twenty-one". This reference is to Decree-Law 401 of 23 September 1982, which regulates the penal regime applicable to young offenders.

This Decree-Law, in its Article I° , states that "this Decree-Law applies to young people who have committed a fact that qualifies as a criminal offence", which does not apply to "young people who are criminally incompetent due to a psychological anomaly".

In German law, the issue of the age of criminal majority is regulated in § 3° of the Juvenile

67 UNICEF. **Special Protections Progress & Disparity:** Old enough to be a criminal? Available at: <http://www.unicef.org/pon97/p56a.htm>. Accessed on: 19 August 2011.

68MAHER, Gerry. Age and Criminal Responsibility. **Ohio State Journal of Criminal Law,** Columbus, v. 2, p. 493-512, 2005. Available at: <http://moritzlaw.osu.edu/osjcl/Articles/Volume2_2/Symposium/Maher-PDF-4-ll-05.pdf>. Accessed on: 19 August 2011.

Court Act (Jugendgerichtsgesetz), which states that "an adolescent is legally responsible when at the time of the event he was sufficiently mature, according to his moral and mental development, to understand the wrongfulness of the act committed and to act on the basis of this understanding". It thus takes into account the question of discernment when committing offences.

Paragraph 19 of the German Penal Code (Strafgesetzbuch) also provides for criminal imputability at the age of fourteen, thus creating special protection like the other laws already studied. Claus Roxin teaches about this provision :[69] [70]

> *It is correct to estimate that this is a regulation of the exclusion of responsibility that can be based either on the fact that the child was still not normatively acceptable or on the fact that there is no preventive need for punishment. Life experience teaches us that older children, for the most part, know perfectly well that smashing windows, hurling, etc., is not allowed. Sometimes children are also in a situation where they can be motivated by these prohibitions, so that guilt itself would have to be affirmed. However, as the actions of children do not change the collective legal consciousness in the eyes of adults, and as the imposition of criminal sanctions against children is especially contraindicated, the legislator has rightly excluded responsibility.*[71]

Accordingly, Paulo José da Costa Júnior teaches[72] that "[...] the *Jugendstrafrecht* was created by the law of 4 August 1973. It is aimed at minors between the ages of fourteen and eighteen and, under certain conditions, also at young people between the ages of eighteen and twenty-one. Minors under the age of fourteen are entrusted to welfare law."

With regard to Islamic law, using Iran as a reference, Shirin Ebadi, winner of the Nobel Peace Prize in 2003 and a human rights activist, in an interview with Jornal do Advogado[73] , said that

---

[69]"At first glance, the set age seems low. However, one might think that children are developing at a faster rate than before. Today, eight-year-olds have a greater understanding of the world (certainly due to technology) than seven-year-olds did in the 18th and 19th centuries (when the rule was established in Scots law). This may then suggest that there could be a reduction in the age in the Scottish paradigm, from eight years old to a lower age." Our translation.

[70] ROXIN, Claus. **Criminal Law General Part: Volume L Foundations. The structure of criminal theory.** Madrid: Thomson Civitas, 2003. p. 847/848. Translated by Diego-Manuel Luzón Pena, Miguel Díaz y Garcia Conlledo and Javier de Vicente Remesal.

[71] "It's correct to think that this is a rule excluding responsibility that can be based on the fact that the child is not normatively prepared or that there is no need for preventive punishment. Life experience teaches older children that they often know very well that breaking stones in windows, stealing, etc. is not allowed. Often the children are also in a position to motivate themselves for these prohibitions, so that guilt would be asserted by them. But since children's actions do not move the collective legal conscience of adults, and the imposition of preventive criminal sanctions against children is thwarted, the legislator has rightly excluded responsibility. - Our translation.

[72] COSTA JÚNIOR, Paulo José da. **Comentários ao código penal.** 6. ed. current. São Paulo: Saraiva, 2009. p. 121.

[73] EBADI, Shirin. Interview. **Lawyer's Journal.** LAWYER'S NEWSPAPER. **Interview.** São Paulo. Year XXXVII. n. 363, July 2011. Available at:
<http://www2.oabsp.org.br/asp//jomal/default.asp>. Accessed on 23 August 2011.

Iranian legislation, after the 1979 Revolution, established the age of criminal majority at nine for girls and fifteen for boys. In this way, young people over the above age will be held criminally responsible for the offence as if they were adults.

In addition, Shirin Ebadi criticised the Iranian sentencing system, which provides for the execution of minors under the age of eighteen.

Spanish legislation, on the other hand, establishes in Article 19 of the Penal Code that "minors under the age of eighteen shall not be criminally liable under the terms of this Code". In fact, Spanish law, like Brazilian law, stipulates that in cases of offence, young people will be held accountable to the law, i.e. they will not go unpunished.

Jesús-María Silva Sánchez[74] , teaches that "[...] *young minors - those in the 16-18 age bracket - remain subject to the state's punitive power in a similar way to adults, although benefiting from a significant reduction in punishment."*[15]

It is important to emphasise that previous Spanish legislation provided for the age of criminal majority at sixteen. A. Quintano Ripolles[75] [76] teaches that the issue of immaturity, i.e. the fact that young people up to the age of sixteen had no real understanding of the illegality of their actions, meant that they were considered to be unimputable. It was believed that, just like an adult who had some mental pathology that made them incapable of discerning between right and wrong, adolescents under the age of sixteen were also considered so.

Italian law allows adolescents between the ages of fourteen and eighteen to be considered imputable. This is because this legislation has adopted the biopsychological criterion and, in this way, the intellectual-volitional capacity of the young person will be ascertained when the offence is committed, thus assessing their capacity for discernment.

José da Costa Júnior teaches[77] that "[...] from fourteen to eighteen, in the Italian system, minors are considered imputable, if they have the capacity to understand and will. But the penalty will be reduced." Thus, the young person will be held accountable for the act committed, being considered imputable, for which they will be subjected to an assessment to ascertain whether or not they had discernment about their actions at the time of the offence.

---

[74] SÁNCHEZ, Jesús-Maria Silva. La política criminal ante el hecho penalmente antijurídico cometido por un menor de edad. In. FRANCO, Alberto Silva; Nucci, Guilherme de Souza. **Criminal Law.** São Paulo: Ed. Revistas dos Tribunais, 2010. v. 7. p. 759.

[75] "... young minors - between the ages of 16-18 - remain subject to the punitive power of the state in a similar way to adults, but benefit from a significant mitigation of the penalty imposed on them. Our translation.

[76] RIPOLLES, A. Quintano. **Comentários al código penal.** Madrid: Revista del Derecho Privado Madrid, 1966. p.

[77] COSTA JÚNIOR, Paulo José da. **Comentários ao código penal.** 6. ed. current. São Paulo: Saraiva, 2009. p. 120.

The author[78] also explains that:

> "Minors are tried in Italy by a specialised court: the 'Tribunale per i minorenni'. On the other hand, minors will benefit from the application of judicial pardon or pecuniary penalty, when the custodial sentence does not exceed three years; from conditional release, which can be ordered by the minister at any time during the execution of the penal sanction; from rehabilitation, which is granted when the minor shows good behaviour, as well as other benefits, provided for in successive laws on criminal law, criminal procedure and penitentiary law, which form the so-called criminal law of minors."

Regarding the French model of the age of criminal majority, René Gerraud teaches[79] that although France has established the age of criminal majority at eighteen, there are some particularities that differentiate it from other foreign legal systems, including the model adopted by Brazil in the Statute of the Child and Adolescent.

This legislation takes into account the fact that the young person, when committing an offence, has committed it with due discernment, i.e. before even worrying about proving that the adolescent is the perpetrator of the offence, it must be shown that at the time of the offence, they had sufficient understanding to know that their conduct was contrary to the law.

Thus, when investigating the commission of offences by minors under the age of eighteen, it is extremely important to assess whether they had discernment of their actions, and this proof is the responsibility of the Public Prosecutor's Office. It should be emphasised that, even if the materiality and authorship of the offence by the adolescent are proven, if it is not proven that they acted with the proper discernment, they will be acquitted, but if appropriate, some educational measure will be applied.

The French model also has two characteristics that are worth highlighting. The first concerns young people under the age of sixteen who, because of their age, have a special privilege when it comes to the application of a "penalty". Thus, if they are convicted and it is proven that they acted with discernment, they will benefit from a mitigating factor. Young people between the ages of sixteen and eighteen, however, if their understanding of the act is proven, will be held accountable as if they were adults.

In this model, adolescents under the age of sixteen are held accountable for offences before specialised courts, following a faster and simpler procedure than other criminals.

However, there are three exceptions to this rule. The first occurs when the offence is committed in co-authorship with people over the age of sixteen, in which case they will be tried in the Criminal Court *(cour d'assissesy)*; the second occurs when the offence is of a serious nature, i.e.

---

[78] Ibid.

[79] GERARUD, René. **Compendium of criminal law.** Campinas: LZN, 2003. Vol. I. p. 259-268.

due to the seriousness of the act committed, the young person will be tried in the Criminal Court; and finally, the third occurs when a press crime is committed, in which case the adolescent will be tried in their own jurisdiction.

René Gerraud[80] believes, however, that establishing an age at which young people become aware of their actions is difficult, as each person matures at a different time. Life experiences, education and access to information mean that young people, through contact with the world, develop and become able to answer for their actions.

It should also be noted that the Rome Statute of the International Criminal Court[81] in article 26 deals with the "Exclusion of Jurisdiction over Persons under the Age of 18", stating that "The Court shall not have jurisdiction over persons who, at the time of the alleged commission of the offence, have not attained the age of eighteen years". This exclusion is due to international negotiations at the United Nations level, which stipulated that imputability begins at the age of eighteen and that, from this point onwards, it is reasonable for young people to be held criminally responsible for their actions. This statute was introduced into Brazilian law by Decree 4388 of 25 September 2002.

It is important to emphasise that, regardless of the age established as the starting point for the age of criminal responsibility, the various countries mentioned have their own rules that provide special treatment for children and adolescents, which are in line with international treaties on the subject. Thus, although the ages vary in each state, young people are treated as physically and intellectually developing persons.

2.2.1 Comparison between the Canadian model and the ECA

Alex Eduardo Gallo and Lúcia C. de Albuquerque Williams[82] , in a study carried out in 2004, compared the treatment of young people in Brazil and Canada. To this end, two medium-sized cities were chosen so that the proposed work could be carried out using similar paradigms: São Carlos, in the interior of São Paulo, and London, a city in the south of the province of Ontario.

The authors were concerned to show that, despite the data collected, it should be analysed in the light of the political, economic and socio-cultural differences between Brazil and Canada. By way of illustration, it should be noted that in Canada, touching another person's buttocks is considered

---

[80] GERRAUD, René. **Compendium of criminal law.** Campinas: LZN, 2003. Vol. I. p. 266-269.
[81] ROME STATUTE OF THE INTERNATIONAL CRIMINAL COURT. Available at: <http://www2.mre.gov.br/dai/tpi.htm>. Accessed on 06 October 2011.
[82] GALLO, Alex Eduardo; Williams, Lúcia C. Albuquerque. Adolescents in conflict with the law: a comparison between Brazil and Canada. **Revista da Faculdade de Direito da Universidade Federal do Paraná,** n. 49, 2009. p. 141-156.

a crime of sexual offence under local law, whereas such a practice is tolerated in Brazil, and the person is at most warned about their conduct.

Both countries have special legislation regarding children and adolescents. Brazil is regulated by the Statute of the Child and Adolescent and Canada is regulated by a similar law called the *Young Offenders Act,* but both legislations establish different treatment for young people between the ages of twelve and eighteen.

In Canada, despite the fact of special protection, differentiated treatment is adopted with regard to imputability. The age of the child or adolescent does not matter in this legal system, but rather the characteristics of each case. So, for example, if a twelve year old commits a serious crime such as murder, and has a history of offending because he has served several other measures previously, which have not proved to be adequate in their resocialising role, he can be transferred to the Criminal Court and tried as if he were an adult, and may even be sentenced to life imprisonment.

With regard to the measures applied to young offenders, Canada has so-called alternative measures that basically resemble the socio-educational measures established in the ECA. The Canadian model has added two other measures, namely: an apology to the victim, which can take place during the hearing or in writing, and the alternative measure of a fine, which consists of the payment of a sum of money that always exceeds five thousand Canadian dollars.

The investigation of unlawful behaviour in Canadian law has points in common with Brazilian law. However, in the case of non-serious offences, such as verbal aggression by schoolmates, the police may choose not to file a complaint and only take the offender to their guardians, warning them about their actions.

Another difference that deserves to be pointed out is the question of the obligation of a technical defence at the hearing before the judicial authority. While the ECA guarantees a technical defence at the hearing, as well as the appointment of a lawyer in cases where the offender cannot afford to hire a professional, Canadian legislation establishes that if the young person does not have sufficient income to hire a lawyer, they can defend themselves. In this case, they can use the *legal aid* service, which is carried out by a lawyer registered with a government body who will receive funding from the Canadian government for the services rendered, similar to the procedure used in Brazil, regarding the agreement for the provision of services signed with the OAB.

What is also new is the way in which the young person's discernment when committing the offence is investigated. Thus, at the court hearing, the judge can order the teenager to undergo a psychological assessment, which will show whether or not they have discernment about their actions. This assessment is carried out in multidisciplinary centres, in this case at the *Centre for Children and Families in the Justice System of the London Family Court Clinic*, which uses various tools to gain access to school information, family routine, drug use and illnesses through data from a government system, as well as providing support to young people's families.

The medical psychological assessment report will take into account the adolescent's life, i.e. issues relating to their development, social relationships, education, as well as the seriousness of the offence committed. By analysing all these factors, the judge will have sufficient mechanisms to assess whether or not the young person had discernment about the act committed, as well as the best measure to be applied.

It should also be noted that the Canadian system, like the Brazilian model, opts to establish socio-educational measures that, in addition to being punitive and reparative, have a pedagogical character, aimed at demonstrating that the act committed is not in accordance with the law. On this point, Canadian legislation is more efficient, since the specialised centres, as already mentioned, have other activities that supplement the alternative measures imposed on young offenders.

Furthermore, the Canadian model, like the Brazilian one, uses the internment measure as an *ultima ratio,* i.e. it should be applied as a last resort when other measures have not proved effective. On this point, the *Canadian Centre for Justice Statistics*[83] shows that, in 1997, alternative measures were applied in the following proportions: 68 % of adolescents were subject to *probation,* 30 % to *community services*, 20 % to *open custody,* 16 % to *secure custody,* 6 % to *fines* and, in 2 % of cases, the case was closed due to insufficient evidence.

The research carried out by the authors showed that when reading the data presented, as well as the model adopted in both legislations, the political, economic and socio-cultural differences between Brazil and Canada must be taken into account.

Finally, the study showed that Canadian education has better learning rates than Brazilian education, and that young offenders in Canada, as well as their parents, have higher levels of schooling than in Brazil, a factor that directly influences the commission of offences and the return to crime after completing a socio-educational or alternative measure.

2.2.2 English case

In October 2007, a twelve-year-old teenager in the city of Worcester, mid-west England, was accused of engaging in sexual activity with two other young people of the same age, having sexual relations with them consisting of anal penetration, oral sex and masturbation. In his defence, he claimed not to know that what he was doing was "wrong and illegal". In the end, he was convicted and appealed to the House of Lords, the last instance of English justice .[84]

---

[83] CANADIAN CENTRE FOR JUSTICE STATISTICS. **A profile of yoimg justice in Canada.** Ottawa: Minister of Industry Canada, 1998.

[84]HOUSE OF LORDS. Parliamentary business. Publications & records. Lords publications. **Judgment Index.** Available at: <http://www.publications.parliament.uk/pa/ld200809/ldjudgmt/jd090429/jtb- l.htm>. Accessed

At the time, the case had repercussions throughout the United Kingdom, and it was questioned whether or not there should be a change in legislation for children and young people, given that in England the age of majority is ten. The argument used by the teenager, which was also questioned by English scholars, referred to the so-called *doli incapax,* i.e. the teenager argued that due to his age he did not have the capacity to answer criminally for the offence committed.

During the judgement, questions were raised about the evolution of the institute in the British legal system over the years, and the conclusion was reached that, although there was provision in previous legislation for adolescents between the ages of twelve and fourteen to be protected by *doli incapax*, nowadays, given the education provided by the state and access to information, young people should be assessed as to their discernment.

From this perspective, it is worth highlighting the fact that there are two currents of thought regarding the situation described, namely: regarding the abolition of the presumption brought about by the doctrine of *doli incapax*, with this protection ceasing to exist for young people, and regarding the maintenance of the institute, although an assessment should be made of the young person's capacity for discernment when committing the offence.

In this case, the House of Lords, while upholding the teenager's conviction and not accepting the *doli incapax* argument, took a position in favour of the institute claimed by the defence, which was responsible for proving the teenager's volitional incapacity when he committed the criminal offence.

In Brazil, a similar case[85] took place in 2010 in the city of Florianópolis, where two fourteen-year-old teenagers were accused and convicted of raping a thirteen-year-old girl.

At the time, one of the young men met the victim and took her to a friend's house, where after drinking alcohol, they forced the teenager to have sex. Both teenagers were convicted of the offence and given probation, which generated a lot of controversy in society due to the seriousness of the offence, as well as the fact that they belonged to influential families in the region.

Thus, it can be seen from the analysis carried out that, in England, the punishment of children and adolescents is based on the verification of the adolescent's intellectual-volitional capacity when committing an offence, in other words, the need for the young person to have the necessary discernment to be convicted of committing a criminal offence. In Brazil, according to the Constitution and the Statute of the Child and Adolescent, young people under the age of eighteen are responsible for committing offences, but they are given special treatment.

---

on: 08 September 2011.

[85] PEOPLE'S MAIL. **Justice surprises and applies light sentence to rapists in SC.** Available at: <http://www.correiodopovo.com.br/Noticias/?Noticia=181771>. Accessed on: 08 September 2011.

CHAPTER 3

THE AGE OF CRIMINAL RESPONSIBILITY: REDUCTION, MAINTENANCE OR ALTERATION OF THE PARADIGM ADOPTED BY THE BRAZILIAN STATE

3.1 Perspectives on the age of criminal majority

As a treaty, Brazil established eighteen years of age as the starting point for the age of criminal responsibility. In terms of criminal policy and taking into account the biological criterion, when a young person reaches the age of eighteen they are considered criminally responsible if they commit a crime or misdemeanour. Below this age, and being over twelve years of age, if they commit an offence, the adolescent will be held responsible in accordance with the rules laid down in the Statute of the Child and Adolescent.

The commission of serious offences with major repercussions and social commotion has led to the questioning of Brazilian legislation regarding the special treatment guaranteed to children and adolescents. The issue, however, has not been treated with the attention it deserves. The data presented in the first chapter of this study shows that child and adolescent crime has been on the rise in recent years and that the authorities have not been more concerned about this.

In a recent report published on the UOL website[86] , the Institute for Applied Economic Research (IPEA) pointed to a major reduction in investment in programmes related to children and adolescents. The National Socio-Educational Care Programme, for example, had its funding cut by more than three hundred percent, while in 2009 the amount was around 6.1 million reais. In 2010, this amount was reduced to just 1.4 million reais.

This shows a total lack of commitment on the part of the state to the issue of child crime, whether it's the reduction in funding for special programmes or the absence of policies that promote changes or adjustments to the current system.

In view of the study carried out and starting from the historical evolution of the institute, addressing the practical aspects of its application and analysing the criteria adopted to establish the starting point of criminal responsibility, both nationally and internationally, we will begin the study of the proposals for changes with regard to the age established as the starting point of criminal responsibility.

Despite the age limit set by the Penal Code and subsequently enshrined and supported by

[86] MOREIRA, Fabrício Calado. **Federal government increased spending, but some social programmes were reduced, says IPEA.** Available at: <http://noticias.uol.com.br/politica/2011/08/25/govemo- federal-government-increased-spending-but-some-social-programmes-have-reduced-says-ipea.jhtm> Accessed on: 26 August 2011.

the Federal Constitution as a special guarantee of protection for children and adolescents who, because they are developing intellectually and emotionally, need special treatment, this age is highly questioned. This does not mean, in principle, that the age at which criminal responsibility begins should be raised or maintained, nor that it should be lowered. The question that must be asked when analysing the issue is whether young people today, who have broad access to information, need the same protection that was established at the time the criminal legislation on the matter, the Federal Constitution and the ECA were published.

It is clear that Brazilian society has undergone significant changes in just over two decades, given the new realities it has experienced, whether due to technological innovations and the massification of the means of communication, or even due to policies adopted by the state in the face of economic growth, especially in recent years.

At this point, the legal profession, as an integral part of society, should be concerned with its constant updating, although caution should be exercised in order to avoid hasty decisions, which could lead to legal uncertainty. What's more, a complete analysis of the institute could provide information that shows, in advance, the positive and negative points of any change.

It should be noted, however, that the purpose of this study is not to seek alternatives for punishing or decriminalising the conduct of adolescent offenders, not least because they are accountable for their actions under statutory law. The focus of the questioning is whether the age set at eighteen is still adequate to define the age of criminal majority.

It is important, in this matter, that the population shows itself to be aligned with a discourse of legislative change, not least because, in the event of an eventual reduction in the age of criminal responsibility, whatever the age, it must be prepared. In this case, the young person who was previously serving a socio-educational internment measure in a special unit for adolescent offenders will be transferred to the ordinary prison system, intensifying the problems that exist in the national prison system due to overcrowding and lack of structure.

Therefore, before any legislative change is made on this subject, a broad social, economic and cultural study should be carried out, because lowering the age limit will not necessarily mean a reduction in violence rates, but it will directly increase the number of prisoners in Provisional Detention Centres and Penitentiaries.

3.2 . Reducing the Penal Age

With the aim of adapting the legislation for children and adolescents to the country's social reality and in order to meet the popular desire for change, some legal scholars have taken a position in favour of reducing the age of criminal responsibility, believing that lowering the age of criminal responsibility will curb the practice of unlawful acts by children and adolescents and, consequently, reduce violence rates.

As a result, the understanding is that by lowering the established age, young people who previously committed criminal offences and were liable under the rules of the Statute for Children and Adolescents will be inhibited by the stricter penalties when they become liable under criminal law and before the ordinary criminal justice system.

This position is not aimed at applying criminal law *prima facie,* which could distort the entire criminal structure due to the rigour of the punishments provided. On the contrary, it should be seen as the *ultima ratio* and thus applied when other measures are not sufficient to curb criminal behaviour.

In this context, Cezar Roberto Bitencourt[87] teaches that:

> [...] in order to admit a reduction in the age of 'criminal responsibility', competence and seriousness are required, aspects that are not common in the treatment of the Brazilian penal repressive system as a whole. In fact, incompetence and lack of seriousness in dealing with these issues has been the keynote of our political-criminal reality. For this reason, we are even afraid to support this thesis, because the 'legislators on duty' might like the idea, but, as always happens in Brazil, only take advantage of it halfway: adopt this diminished criminal responsibility and 'forget' to create the 'appropriate establishments', exclusively for minors! Furthermore, this thesis cannot be developed satisfactorily in this space.

Thus, despite the fact that part of the doctrine defends lowering the age of criminal responsibility, such a procedure must be preceded by a broad discussion, based on a project that establishes goals to be achieved, since there would be no point in a change if violence against children and young people did not decrease.

One of the existing proposals in this regard envisages lowering the penal age to sixteen. This current is based on the premise that the Federal Constitution, in its article 14, § Iº , inc. II, point c, allows adolescents between the ages of sixteen and eighteen to actively register to vote, even if it is optional, and thus be able to choose their representatives. Thus, it stands to reason that if adolescents of this age have sufficient capacity and discernment to exercise their right to suffrage, then they could also be criminally liable for committing illegal acts.

In this sense, Eder Jorge[88] ponders that there are no logical reasons to support maintaining

[87] BITENCOURT, Cezar Robeerto. **Criminal law manual:** general part. 7. ed. rev. and updated. São Paulo: Saraiva, 2002 vol. 1. p. 307.

[88] ÉDER, JORGE. **Reducing the age of criminal responsibility.** Available at: <http://jus.uol.com.br/revista/texto/3374/reducao-da-maioridade-penal>. Accessed on: 27 August 2011.

the age of criminal majority at eighteen, not least because the legislator has given adolescents, from the age of sixteen, the right to elect their representatives, whether at local level, as in the case of mayors and councillors, or even at national level, such as the President of the Republic, and if they are given the necessary discernment to vote, they should have the same responsibility for committing illicit criminal acts.

Ives Granda da Silva Martins[89] states that the Brazilian legal system presents an incongruity, since "[...] a minor under the age of 16 can decide an election on who should lead the destiny of a nation and is criminally incompetent." He also believes that, at the time the Constitution was drafted, the cultural and social-historical paradigm differed from the present day, justifying setting the age of criminal majority at eighteen. It turns out, however, that the paradigm experienced today, in the face of technological advances, requires adaptations and readjustments to the legislation in force, with a reduction in the starting age for the age of criminal majority.

In this perspective, Guilherme de Souza Nucci[90] teaches that if adolescents from the age of sixteen "[...] become citizens by voting voluntarily [...]", they should also have criminal responsibility, since they are given and guaranteed the proper discernment to choose their representatives and, in this case, they should also have the necessary discernment to understand what they can and cannot do in criminal terms and thus be duly held responsible for their actions.

On this issue, João Batista Costa Saraiva warns :[91]

> To say that if a 16-year-old can vote and can therefore go to jail is a half-truth (or a complete untruth). Voting at 16 is optional, while imputability is compulsory. Moreover, the overwhelming majority of offenders in this age group don't even know about their potential status as voters; they lack awareness and information.

In opposition to these arguments, René Ariel Dotti[92] believes that, despite the fact that adolescents from the age of sixteen have the active capacity to vote and can therefore choose their representatives, this reasoning cannot be used in the criminal field, where adolescents under the age of eighteen have special protection under the ECA.

It should be emphasised that although adolescents have the right to vote at the age of sixteen, they are constitutionally guaranteed the right to receive differentiated treatment because they are at a stage of maturation and physical and intellectual-volitional development.

---

89 MARTINS, Ives Granda da Silva; MENDES, Gilmar Ferreira and DO NACIMENTO, Carlos Valder. **Treatise on constitutional law.** São Paulo: Saraiva, 2010. p. 676.

90 NUCCI, Guilherme de Souza. **Commentary on the Criminal Code.** 9. ed. rev. , atual, e ampl. São Paulo: Revista dos Tribunais, 2008. p. 282.

91 SARAIVA, João Batista Costa. **Reasons for not lowering criminal imputability.** In. FRANCO, Alberto Silva; NUCCI, Guilherme de Souza. (**Criminal Law.** São Paulo: Revista dos Tribunais, 2010. vol. 7. p. 751.

92 DOTTI, René Ariel. **Criminal law course:** general part. Rio de Janeiro: Forense, 2005. p. 412-417.

In this sense, João Batista Costa Saraiva ponders[93] that the legal reference *is* merely a choice made by the constituent when drawing up the Magna Carta, since it set different ages for young people to be able to work, vote, be considered unimputable, among others:

> Incidentally, Brazilian legislation sets various age parameters, and there is no single age at which 'absolute majority' is reached at the same moment. A teenager can work from the age of 14 and, at electoral level, it establishes that a citizen must be at least 18 to run for councillor; 21 for deputy, mayor or justice of the peace; 30 for governor and 35 for president, senator or justice of the supreme court. There is no subjective qualification criterion, but rather a political decision.

Analysing the institute from another perspective, Fernando Capez[94] is in favour of reducing the age of criminal majority, understanding that young people at the age of sixteen have "full capacity for understanding and volition" and should therefore be criminally liable for the crimes committed. He also claims that part of the responsibility should be attributed to the state for failing to provide education and employment opportunities for young people, which would directly contribute to reducing their participation in the criminal world, thus reducing the rates of violence. He also believes that young people serving a socio-educational detention order should not be compulsorily released at the age of 21; on the contrary, they should remain in a detention centre until they reach the age of 30. In this way, when they commit an extremely serious offence, they would be held more strictly accountable, which would prevent adolescents from committing crimes.

The author[95] also believes that statutory legislation regulates rules that encourage violence and disempower society:

> The Statute of the Child and Adolescent (ECA) is a legal affront and, above all, an attack on social justice. This statute encourages criminality through the impunity of underage criminals, since the ECA has the effrontery to prohibit the publicising of their names, and their photos can only be printed with a protection order.

With this, a new paradigm is proposed, in which adolescent offenders who commit serious offences and are sentenced to the socio-educational measure of internment would not be compulsorily released when they reach the age of 21. On the contrary, they would remain in compliance with the imposed measure and could serve it until the age of 30 in their own establishment, created for this

---

[93] SARAIVA, op. cit. p. 752.

[94] CAPEZ, Fernando. **The question of reducing the age of criminal responsibility.** Available at: <http://www.epm.sp.gov.br/Internas/ArtigosView.aspx?ID=3016>. Accessed on: 27 October 2010.

[95] CAPEZ, Fernando. **Criminal law, volume I, general part.** 2 ed. São Paulo: Saraiva, 2001.

purpose.

Another point to be addressed when proposing a possible reduction in the age of criminal majority concerns the fact that this age was established by the constitution as a fundamental right and guarantee of the human person and, as such, this provision is considered a clause that cannot be altered by means of a constitutional amendment or any other legislative initiative.

On this issue, Pedro Lenza, in favour of reducing the age of criminal responsibility, believes that:

> [...] our personal position is that it is perfectly possible to reduce the age from 18 to 16, since only the proposal of an amendment (PEC) tending to abolish individual rights and guarantees is not allowed. This does not mean, as the Supreme Court has already interpreted, that the matter can be changed.[96]

The author also ponders that "by reducing the age of criminal responsibility from 18 to 16, the right to non-punishment, seen as a fundamental guarantee, will not cease to exist."[97] The understanding is that only the starting age for responsibility would be altered, and the institute relating to non-punishment would not be modified or extinguished.

Guilherme de Souza Nucci[98] believes that it is possible to reduce the age of criminal responsibility by amending the Constitution. He also points out that imputability is not included in the list of fundamental rights and guarantees, but in the chapter entitled "The Family, the Child, the Adolescent, the Young Person and the Elderly", which would allow this change. In this sense, he states:

> We can't agree with the thesis that there are fundamental human rights and guarantees that can be found in other parts of the Charter, and therefore also in the "*ironclad clauses*", which are included in the impossibility of amendment provided for in Article 6, § 4° , IV of the FC, because it is known that there are "rights and guarantees of material content" and "rights and guarantees of formal content" [...]. Therefore, not only is the age of criminal majority not a fundamental right in the material sense, in our opinion, it is also not a fundamental right in the formal sense. Therefore, there is no impediment to a constitutional amendment removing or modifying Article 228 of the Constitution.

This doctrinal current defends the idea that the age of criminal majority, although not included in the list of individual rights and guarantees, is also considered a permanent clause and

---

96 LENZA, Pedro. **Direito constitucional esquematizado.** 12. ed. rev., atual, e ampl. São Paulo: Saraiva. 2008. p. 762.

97 Ibid.

98 NUCCI, Guilherme de Souza. **Commentary on the Criminal Code.** 9. ed. rev., atual, e ampl. São Paulo: Ed. Revista dos Tribunais, 2008. p. 282.

therefore cannot be altered by an amendment to the Constitution.

As we have seen, in the face of the social clamour for legislative changes with regard to the commission of offences by adolescents, part of the doctrine has begun to discuss the possibility of reducing the age established as the starting point for criminal responsibility, based on issues relating to the age established for adolescents to be able to exercise their right to citizenship through suffrage, as well as the fact that it is understood that criminal imputability is not part of the list of fundamental rights and guarantees of the person.

3.3 Maintaining the age of majority at eighteen

The Statute of the Child and Adolescent, despite the fact that it set the age of criminal responsibility at eighteen, protects children and adolescents, who are at a stage of development and should receive different treatment to that given to offenders. From this perspective, the Statutory Law should be acclaimed for being one of the most advanced pieces of legislation in the world, above all because its content is in line with the rules advocated at both national and international level.

In this sense, Júlio Fabbrini Mirabete" presents the reduction of the age of criminal responsibility as a "modern trend", however, he teaches that:

> No one can deny that young people aged 16 to 17, from any social background, today have a broad knowledge of the world and the ability to discern the illegality of their actions. However, lowering the age limit in ordinary criminal law would represent a step backwards in Brazilian penal and penitentiary policy and would create promiscuity between young people and habitual offenders. The Statute of the Child and Adolescent provides effective instruments to prevent the repeated commission of illegal acts by people under the age of 18, without the inconveniences mentioned above.

What has been questioned is whether, with the possible reduction of the age of criminal responsibility and the consequent sending of adolescents who were previously interned in their own establishments and would now be part of the Brazilian prison system, there would be a collapse in the prison system.

In a recent speech, Supreme Court Justice Cezar Peluso[99] [100] compared some Brazilian prisons to "medieval dungeons", and asserted that the current model is incapable of re-socialising convicts due to its various deficiencies. The Justice also stated that the Brazilian prison model has

---

[99] MIRABETE, Julio Fabbrini. **Manual of criminal law:** general part. 24. ed. rev. and updated. São Paulo: Atlas, 2008. vol. 1. p. 214.

[100] PAGNAN, Rogério. **STF president compares prisons to medieval dungeons.** Available at:<http://wwwl .folha.uol.com.br/cotidiano/894132-presidente-do-stf-compara-prisoes-a-masmorras- medievais.shtml>. Accessed on 24 September 2011.

failed.

In a report published by Folha Online[101] , data from a report drawn up by the International Bar Association showed that there are various irregularities in the Brazilian prison system, ranging from overcrowding in prisons, lack of infrastructure and poor sanitary conditions, to violence and security problems.

It is clear that the purpose of sentencing has not been fulfilled. Brazil adopts the so-called mixed theory of punishment and, according to Edgar Magalhães Noronha[102] "[...] punishment has a retributive nature, but aims at the re-education of the criminal and general intimidation. He therefore affirms the retributive nature of the penalty, but accepts its utilitarian function." Guilherme de Souza Nucci considers that punishment is "[...] the sanction imposed by the State, through criminal action, on the criminal, whose purpose is retribution for the offence perpetrated and the prevention of new crimes."[103] Edilson Mougenot Bonfim and Fernando Capez understand that punishment is the "[...] restriction or deprivation of a legal asset, the purpose of which is to apply punitive retribution to the offender, promote their social rehabilitation and prevent further offences by intimidating the community."[104]

Luís Fernando Camargo de Barros Vidal[105] believes that if the age established as the starting point for the age of criminal responsibility is lowered, this change will do nothing to reduce the rate of offences by adolescents, since it will only have repercussions in the punitive sphere and not in the re-education or reintegration of adolescents into society. In this sense:

> The worst blind person, as the popular saying goes, is the one who doesn't want to see. As in José Saramago's fiction (Essay on Blindness), the advocates of the radical solution of imprisonment don't realise that the causes of evil remain latent and operative beyond the walls of confinement, and that no one, inside or outside prisons, will be immune to its effects.

In the same context, Carlos Eduardo Barreiros Rebelo[106] , considers that:

---

101 MONTEIRO, André. **Prisons and criminal justice in Brazil are dysfunctional, says report.** Available at: <http://wwwl.folha.uol.com.br/folha/cotidiano/ult95u722246.shtml>. Accessed on 24 September 2011.

102 NORONHA, E. Magalhães. **Criminal law:** introduction and general part. 38. ed. revised and updated. São Paulo: Saraiva, 2004. vol. 1. p. 226.

103 NUCCI, Guilherme de Souza. **Criminal law manual:** general and special parts. 6. ed. revised, updated and expanded. São Paulo: Ed. Revista dos Tribunais, 2009. p. 379.

104 BONFIM, Edilson Mougenot; CAPEZ, Fernando. **Criminal law:** general part. São Paulo: Saraiva, 2004.p.633.

105 VIDAL, Luís Fernando Camargo de Barros. The criminal irresponsibility of adolescents. In FRANCO, Alberto Silva; NUCCI, Guilherme de Souza. (Org.) **Criminal Law.** São Paulo: Ed. Revista dos Tribunais, 2010. vol. 7. p. 795.

106 REBELO, Carlos Eduardo Barreiros. **The controversy over reducing the age of criminal**

> Believing that reducing the age of criminal responsibility could be a viable alternative to public safety is, in essence, a distorted and minimalist view of the issue. Prisons are crime factories, because prison overcrowding represents a negative aspect in terms of the repercussions in the sphere of education, rehabilitation and re-socialisation of prisoners.

From this perspective, reducing the age of criminal responsibility would do nothing to reduce the rates of violence and crime, since adolescent offenders would be given the *status of* common criminals and, as a result, when they commit criminal offences they would be inserted into the prison system, which is overcrowded and in no condition to receive new prisoners, let alone young people who need special care.

Carlos Eduardo Barreiros Rebelo[107] warns that:

> It should not be forgotten that overcrowding in prisons is a reality that would be fatally aggravated by reducing the age of criminal responsibility, as prison conditions are insufficient to meet the growing demand for prisoners. Thus, reducing the age of majority seen in isolation could, instead of representing a solution to the problem of public safety, add more ingredients to its worsening.

There are also a number of other arguments in favour of maintaining criminal responsibility at the age of eighteen, such as the fact that the age of criminal majority is considered a fundamental clause, the differentiated treatment guaranteed in the Federal Constitution and regulated by the ECA, the fact that people up to the age of eighteen are still developing physically and psychologically and therefore do not have the proper discernment over their actions, among others.

José Afonso da Silva teaches[108] that the criminal imputability of minors under the age of eighteen is considered a permanent clause, even though it is topologically outside the list contained in art. 5° of the Federal Constitution and, therefore, could not be changed by constitutional amendment, in view of the provisions of § 4° , inc. IV, of art. 60 of the FC.

Accordingly, René Ariel Dotti teaches :[109]

> The unimputability thus declared constitutes one of the fundamental guarantees of the human person, although topographically it is not included in the respective Title (II) of the Constitution that regulates the matter. It is one of the individual rights listed in art. 5° , thus characterising a permanent clause. Consequently, the guarantee cannot be the subject of a constitutional

responsibility. Belo Horizonte: lus, 2010. p. 55.

[107] REBELO, Carlos Eduardo Barreiros. **The age of criminal majority and the controversy over its reduction.** Belo Horizonte: Jus, 2010. p. 55.

[108] DA SILVA, José Afonso. **Contextual commentary on the Constitution.** 5. ed. São Paulo: Malheiros, 2008. p. 864.

[109] DOTTI, René Ariel. **Criminal law course:** general part. Rio de Janeiro: Forense, 2001. p. 412- 413.

> amendment aimed at abolishing it in order to reduce criminal capacity to a lower age limit - sixteen, for example, as has been rumoured. This is opposed by the rule in § 4° , IV, of art. 60 of the FC.

The same position is adopted by Carlos Eduardo Barreiros Rebelo[110] , who believes that the age of criminal majority dealt with in art. 228 of the Federal Constitution, although it was inserted outside the list of individual rights and guarantees, is still part of it, because art. 5° is not an exhaustive list, and there are other individual rights and guarantees throughout the text of the Political Charter.

Alyrio Cavallieri[111] , in favour of maintaining the age of criminal responsibility at eighteen, presents a different perspective on the issue. He proposes that, when referring to young offenders, the expression "irresponsibility" should be used instead of "unimputability", since young people at the age of eighteen, and even younger than that, "[...] know what they are doing [...]". Thus, he teaches that in order for adolescents to be criminally responsible, they must have the capacity for guilt, and "[...] minors have the capacity for guilt (let's leave aside the presumption), but they are not responsible [...]. They know what they're doing, but they don't go to jail, because we have a better solution for their crimes."

In this context, Emilio Garcia Mendez[112] believes that the Statute of the Child and Adolescent is the most advanced legislation in terms of child and adolescent treatment in Latin America, but he still considers it a "concrete utopia". He believes that the Statute can only be fully implemented and thus fulfil its role if there is mutual participation from all sectors of society. Thus, it is up to the state to direct public policies aimed at its full implementation, as well as popular support in overseeing such measures.

In this view, the Statute of the Child and Adolescent has sufficient mechanisms to deal with the issue of child and adolescent crime. However, it questions the role of the state, which, through criminal and social policies, should commit itself to reducing inequalities by investing heavily in education, health and improving people's living conditions. What's more, taking teenagers off the streets or out of detention centres and into the prison system would only make the problem worse.

Luís Fernando Camargo de Barros Vidal[113] evaluates that "[...] the proposal makes clear the attempt to establish a so-called transfer policy, whereby adolescents who are accused of committing a criminal offence are subject to special or common jurisdiction depending on the degree of their

---

[110] REBELO, Carlos Eduardo Barreiros. **The age of criminal majority and the controversy over its reduction.** Belo Horizonte: Jus, 2010. p. 51.

[111] CAVALLIERI, Alyrio. **Flaws in the Statute for Children and Adolescents.** Rio de Janeiro: Forense, 1995. p. 54-56.

[112] MENDEZ, Emílio Garcia; DA COSTA, Antônio Carlos Gomes. **From Needs to Rights.** São Paulo: Malheiros, 1994. p.62.

[113] VIDAL, Luís Fernando Camargo de Barros. **The criminal irresponsibility of adolescents.** In FRANCO, Alberto Silva; NUCCI, Guilherme de Souza. (**Criminal Law.** São Paulo: Revista dos Tribunais, 2010. vol. 7. p. 813.

development."

The Supreme Court Justices Ellen Gracie and Carlos Ayres Britto are also defenders of the current legislation for children and adolescents. In an interview published on the UOL website[114] , they believe that reducing the age of criminal responsibility is not the answer to reducing violence. On the contrary, they emphasise the need for greater agility in judging cases, as well as the application of more appropriate penalties for both common criminals and adolescent offenders.

João Batista da Costa Saraiva believes that the Statute of the Child and Adolescent has sufficient mechanisms to hold adolescents responsible when they commit offences:

> In fact, the argument of the heralds of relegation is fallacious. The Statute offers ample mechanisms for holding these adolescent offenders accountable, and what we have seen, on many occasions, is that while the adolescent co-author has been deprived of his liberty, tried and sentenced and is serving a sentence, his partner who is guilty has often not even had his trial concluded and is often at liberty.[115]

That said, the Statute of the Child and Adolescent has sufficient means to reintegrate young people who commit offences into society, and the procedure regulated by the Statute is faster and more effective in responding to criminal offences. The fact is, however, that it is often applied in the wrong way, either

due to a lack of structure, or even ignorance or disregard on the part of the authorities.

Another criticism of the possible legislative change is that the ECA has not even been properly implemented, so changing the paradigm to include an age below eighteen as the benchmark for criminal responsibility is premature and does not deserve any support.

In this sense, Gláucia Régia Molaz Marins Simões[116] considers that:

> It wouldn't be fair to try to reduce the age of criminal responsibility without first ensuring that the measures laid down in the ECA are implemented, because the ECA is aimed at children and adolescents and if we don't believe in their recovery and reintegration into society, it's a sign that we no longer believe in man himself.

---

[114] GUERREIRO, Gabriela. **President of the Supreme Court says he is against reducing the age of criminal responsibility.** Available at: <http://wwwl.folha.uol.com.br/folha/cotidiano/ult95ul31528.shtml>. Accessed on: 28 August 2011.

[115] SARAIVA, João Batista Costa. **Reasons for not lowering criminal imputability.** In FRANCO, Alberto Silva; NUCCI, Guilherme de Souza. Direito penal, (Org.). São Paulo: Revista dos Tribunais, 2010. vol. 7. p. 746-749.

[116] SIMÕES, Gláucia Régia Molaz Martins. Would lowering the age of criminal responsibility solve the problem of violence? **Legal Journal of the University of Franca.** Franca, year 4, n. 6, p. 77-82, 2001.

João Batista Costa Saraiva[117] ponders that "[...] what we need is a commitment to the full implementation of the Statute of the Child and Adolescent at all levels [...] enforcing this instrument of citizenship and accountability - for adults and young people."

The author[118] also teaches that "The Statute of the Child and Adolescent offers a response to society's just desires for security and, at the same time, seeks to return to society people capable of properly exercising their rights and duties as citizens."

From this perspective, Maria Fernanda Perez and Guilherme de Assis Almeida[119] , members of the Centre for the Study of Violence at the University of São Paulo, believe that the best option with regard to the treatment of children and adolescents would be the effective application of the ECA. They emphasise that policies should be created to encourage improvements in the judicial system, the Public Prosecutor's Office and the police, as well as stating that the consequent reduction in social inequality seems to be the best instrument to be used to reduce violence against children and adolescents.

Along the same lines of understanding about maintaining the age of criminal majority at eighteen and the consequent effective application of the ECA, a new doctrinal discussion has arisen regarding the creation of a Code for the Execution of Socio-Educational Measures. At this point, it is worth highlighting the enactment of Law No. 12,594 of 18 January 2012, which established the National System for Socio-Educational Assistance (SINASE).

Through this, it was possible to regulate some points not dealt with by the Statute of the Child and Adolescent, such as: establishing competences for the federated entities with regard to action in socio-educational programmes, evaluation and monitoring of the management of socio-educational care, accountability of managers, operators and care entities, among others.

It is important to note, however, that this legislation did little to address the fulfilment and execution of socio-educational measures, regulating only points such as the right to visit, including intimate visits, suspension of the execution of the socio-educational measure in cases where the adolescent has mental disorders, judicial decree of internment-sanction after due legal process, among others. With this, it failed to regulate a gap left by statutory legislation, which had not existed until then.

Thus, despite the fact that the legislation laid down in the ECA is complied with and obeyed,

---

117 SARAIVA, João Batista Costa. **Reasons for not lowering criminal imputability.** In FRANCO, Alberto Silva; NUCCI, Guilherme de Souza. Direito penal, (Org.). São Paulo: Revista dos Tribunais, 2010. vol. 7. p. 755.

118 Ibid.

119 SALLA, Thiago Mio; LEOMIL, Leonardo. **Experts question the reduction of the age of criminal responsibility.** Available at: <http://www.4usp.usp.br/index.php/ciencias/11142>. Accessed on: 27 October 2010.

when a teenager is convicted of committing an offence and the socio-educational measure of internment is applied, the term will be indefinite. This can lead to a certain authoritarianism on the part of the judge who, when handing down the sentence for the adolescent's internment, does not set a time limit, i.e. the adolescent could remain in custody for one day or even three years.

In this sense, Alexandre Morais da Rosa[120] argues that the fact that there is no clear law on the rights and guarantees of adolescents in compliance with a socio-educational measure gives both the judge and the people responsible for overseeing compliance wide discretion:

> The programmes for the implementation of socio-educational measures should have clear proposals for action [...]. The Socio-educational Measures Enforcement Bill currently being processed may be a step forward, but it is also linked, at least in the bill, to the desires of the Positivist School and normalisation. [...] The idea is to encourage and assist in the constitution of the subject, promoting, if there is a demand from the adolescent, social referrals (courses, technical training, potentiality, etc.),
> without forcing him to carry out the activities, because otherwise he'll assume the position of a scoundrel. It often happens in a 'fool me, I like you' kind of way. The adolescent knows what they need to say to extinguish the socio-educational measure and the operators of the system imaginatively claim that the pedagogical interest has been fulfilled. And yet another process is extinguished in the name of efficiency.

In this perspective, Mauro Ferrandin[121] believes that the legislation for children and adolescents will only be complete when there is a law regulating the application of socio-educational measures, establishing the criteria for their fulfilment and limiting the discretion of judges, which can generate "extreme legal uncertainty".

Naul Luis Felca teaches[122] that:

> There is no way to work with the procedural tools of the classic branches of law. There are nuances that are completely foreign to the work carried out with children and young people and, no matter how hard legal operators try, there are gaps in both the civil and criminal spheres that go beyond the hermetic system of action, even if they make use of analogy and other phenomena of legislative integration.

Another point that must be taken into consideration is that adolescents up to the age of

---

[120] DA ROSA, Alexandre Morais. Applying the Child and Adolescent Statute. FRANCO, Alberto Silva; NUCCI, Guilherme de Souza. (**Criminal law.** São Paulo: Ed. Revista dos Tribunais, 2010. vol. 7. p. 636.

[121] FERRANDIN, Mauro. **Juvenile criminal act:** applicability of the principles and guarantees of the criminal act. Curitiba: Juruá, 2009. p. 86-87.

[122] FELCA, Naul Luiz. Constituição de 1988: divisor d'águas da infância e juventude, fri **Constituição federal: avanços, contribuições e modificações no processo democrático brasileiro.** São Paulo: Ed. Revista dos tribunais: Centro de Extensão Universitária, 2008. p. 832.

eighteen are in a phase of development and physical and psychological maturation, and penalising them as if they were adults could lead to serious problems.

Carlos Eduardo Barreiros Rebelo[123] argues that:

> Those in favour of maintaining the age of criminal responsibility at 18 use as their main foundation the fact that there is an inherent immaturity in people under the age of 18, since their minds and ethical and moral values are still being formed. Because they are in this phase of changing values, it is argued that it would be possible to correct any misrepresentations they may have suffered and return them to social life without the need for segregation as severe as that imposed on those over 18.

Luiz Augusto Coutinho[124] notes that the vast majority of countries that have adopted criminal policies establishing the age of criminal responsibility below eighteen have not seen a reduction in the levels of violence against children and young people. An example of this is the case of England, where, in accordance with its legislation, children are criminally liable for committing heinous crimes from the age of ten.

Carlos Eduardo Barreiros Rebelo [125] ponders that "[...] reducing the age of criminal responsibility does not solve the problems related to the growth of crime, since, as previously stated, the escalation of violence is much more due to social problems [...]."

In this context, Fernando Andrade Femandes teaches[126] that:

> [...] the question of a legal-penal rationale, the reduction of the age of criminal majority should be firmly denied, because it is not justified in criminological terms, it is not appropriate from a political-criminal perspective and there is no dogmatic reason to support it.

It should also be borne in mind that simply transferring adolescents from detention centres to the ordinary prison system will do nothing to reduce the rate of violence; on the contrary, it will make their situation even worse.

---

[123] REBELO, Carlos Eduardo Barreiros. **The age of criminal responsibility and the controversy over its reduction.**

[124] COUTINHO, Luiz Augusto. **The retrograde step of reducing criminal responsibility to 16 years**. Available at: <http://jus.uol.com.br/revista/texto/4218/retrocesso-da-reducao-da-imputabilidade- penal-para-16-anos>. Accessed on: 28 August 2011.

[125] REBELO, op. cit., p. 68.

[126]FERNANDES, Fernando Andrade. On the legal-penal rationality of reducing the age of criminal responsibility. In. **Public Law Themes.** Jaboticabal: Funep, 2009. p. 73.

Ney Moura Teles[127] states that:

> Wanting to change the penal minimum age in order to imprison teenagers is, unfortunately, wanting to turn them into real, dangerous criminals sooner and more effectively, because sending them to prisons, to socialise with trained, experienced criminals, is giving up any chance of educating them for a dignified life.

Mário Luiz Ramidoff[128] considers that reducing the age of criminal responsibility is "[...] a political-ideological setback for the fundamental rights of children and young people." Furthermore, the author states that the stipulation of an age at which the intellectual-volitional maturity of adolescents is presumed, at international level, is adequate and effective.

Emilio Garcia Mendez[129] considers that:

> *From the point of view of its substantive contents, and I would like this point to be absolutely clear, the Child and Adolescent Statute constitutes an adequate, efficient response that is in line with the highest international standards of respect for human rights. The Child and Adolescent Statute fulfils the double legitimate requirement of simultaneously ensuring the collective security of society with strict respect for the guarantees of individuals regardless of age.*[130]

Having said that, it should be emphasised that the proposed constitutional amendment No. 83 of 2011 is currently being debated[131] , which would reduce the age of criminal and civil majority to sixteen, as well as making it compulsory to vote at that age.

The justification for this proposal is basically based on the institutes we have already studied, i.e. the question is raised about the intellectual-volitional development of young people today compared to the early 1990s. It has been shown that technological development, especially with regard to the media, has meant that today's children and adolescents have more information and are therefore maturing more quickly.

---

[127] TELES, Ney Moura. **Criminal Law:** general part - arts. I° to 120. São Paulo: Atlas, 2004. vol. 1. p. 287-288.

[128] RAMIDOFF, Mário Luiz. **Lições de direito da criança e do adolescente.** 2. ed. rev. e atual. Curitiba: Juruá, 2011. p.169.

[129] MENDEZ, Emilio Garcia. Adolescents and criminal responsibility. In FRANCO, Alberto Silva; NUCCI, Guilherme de Souza. (**Criminal Law.** São Paulo: Ed. Revista dos Tribunais, 2010. vol 7. p. 695.

[130] "From the point of view of its substantive content, and I want this point to be absolutely clear, the Statute for Children and Adolescents constitutes an efficient and appropriate response in line with the highest international standards of respect for human rights. The Statute for Children and Adolescents combines a legitimate demand to guarantee the collective security of society with strict respect for the guarantees of individuals, regardless of their age." - Our translation.

[131]BRAZIL. **Proposed amendment to the Constitution No. 83 of 2011.** Available at: <http://www.senado.gov.br/atividade/materia/getPDF.asp?t=95505&tp=l>. Accessed on: 11 September 2011.

From this perspective, Guilherme de Souza Nucci[132] argues that:

> [...] it is not the reduction of the age of criminal responsibility that will solve the problem of the increase in criminal behaviour in the country, although from a technical and penal point of view, it would be advisable for this to happen in order to adapt the criminal law to reality. Minors under the age of 18 are no longer the same as they were at the beginning of the century, and they don't deserve to continue being treated as people who have no idea of the illicit nature of what they do or fail to do, without being able to conduct themselves in accordance with that understanding.

João Batista Costa Saraiva shares a similar view[133] :

> [...] reforming the Federal Constitution to reduce the age of criminal responsibility, currently set at 18, is a step backwards, a disservice, a real attack. Growing child criminality must be combated at its source - poverty and lack of education. It won't be by throwing 16-year-olds into the failing prison system that they can be rehabilitated. Society has a duty to invest even in those with a difficult prognosis for recovery, not least because the percentage of those who make amends - within the correct execution of the measure that was applied - is much higher and fully justifies the effort. If we don't think like this, tomorrow we will be questioning the reduction of criminal responsibility to twelve years and then to less, who knows, until one day there will be no shortage of people justifying the punishment of the unborn, preferably if they are poor...].

This highlights the need for legislative changes, either to adapt existing rules to new legal and social realities or to change paradigms. However, it is necessary to have a wide-ranging assessment and discussion of the changes to be implemented. Thus, when dealing with the issue of the age of criminal responsibility and the possible alteration of the model adopted by the Brazilian state, a broad study should be carried out, involving the different areas of human knowledge, on the institute, so that there is a secure basis for the legislative results.

---

[132] NUCCI, Guilherme de Souza. **Commentary on the Criminal Code.** 9. ed. rev., atual, e ampl. São Paulo: Ed. Revista dos Tribunais, 2008. p. 282.

[133] SARAIVA, João Batista Costa. **Reasons for not lowering criminal imputability.** In FRANCO, Alberto Silva; NUCCI, Guilherme de Souza. (**Criminal Law.** São Paulo: Ed. Revista dos Tribunais, 2010. vol. 7. p. 755-756.

CHAPTER 4

FINAL CONSIDERATIONS

This paper addressed the issue of violence against children and adolescents, highlighting the question of a possible change in Brazilian legislation regarding the criminal liability of children and adolescents.

From the data presented in the first chapter, it can be seen that child and adolescent crime rates have increased, as has the number of adolescents serving socio-educational sentences, especially in the closed system. It also shows that the treatment given to young offenders has changed over the years, with the current Federal Constitution and the Statute of the Child and Adolescent having brought in the innovative doctrine of integral protection, which protects children and adolescents because they are at an intellectually-volitional stage of development.

Brazil has adopted the biological criterion for defining the age of majority, i.e. from the age of eighteen, adolescents are held criminally responsible for their actions, a choice based on the criminal policy adopted by the Brazilian state.

Foreign legal systems, in comparison with the Brazilian model, mostly adopt the psychological criterion, which takes into account whether or not the adolescent has the necessary discernment when committing the offence, or the biopsychological criterion in which, although an age is set as a reference, the adolescent is analysed on the basis of their discernment when committing the offence.

Analysing the various doctrinal positions on the starting point of the age of criminal responsibility leads to the understanding that reducing the age of criminal responsibility does not seem to be the way forward for reducing violence rates.

Simply holding adolescents from the age of sixteen or any other age criminally responsible will do no good in tackling this violence, since the cause of this criminality will not be tackled.

The best alternative, it can be concluded, would be to maintain the current paradigm. However, the Statute of the Child and Adolescent should be fully implemented, including the creation of a Code for the Execution of Socio-Educational Measures.

This would enable more effective monitoring of compliance with the educational measure imposed, whatever it may be. What's more, legislation of its own would be able to regulate the assessment criteria for adolescents in compliance with a socio-educational measure, since, as has been shown, there has been no law regulating the issue so far, requiring legal operators to work through analogy and other forms of supplementary interpretation.

Thus, as the study has shown, the Statute of the Child and Adolescent has sufficient mechanisms to hold the adolescent responsible for committing an offence, requiring only full implementation of its rules, as well as the aid of public policies aimed at reducing poverty, misery and unemployment rates, in addition to major investment in education.

ANNEXES

ANNEX I

Offences	TOTAL		Inside		Capitals	
	Quotes	(%)	Quotes	(%)	Quotes	(%)
Theft	10717	25,4	2982	15.9	7735	32.9
Theft	7144	16.9	4816	25,7	2328	9.9
Drug trafficking	3504	8.3	1580	8,4	1924	8.2
Illegal possession of weapons	2146	5.1	694	3,7	1452	6,2
Bodily injury	1727	4.1	1109	5,9	618	2.6
Attempted robbery	1521	3.6	207	1,1	1314	5,6
Drug use/possession/entorpcccntcs	1122	27	750	4,0	372	1.6
Homicide	982	2.3	407	2.2	575	2,4
Attempted theft	802	1.9	281	1,5	521	2.2
Threats	780	1.8	462	2,5	318	1.4
Damage	743	1.8	489	2.6	254	1.1
Attempted murder	557	1.3	179	1.0	378	1.6
Driving without a licence	496	1,2	383	2,0	113	0,5
Reception	438	1,0	219	!,2	219	0.9
Criminal offences	358	0,8	292	1,2	66	0.3
Other offences	3005	7.1	2103	11.2	902	3.8
Not available	6173	14.6	1757	9.4	4416	18.8

Source: Hanud. Pesquisa Mapeamento Nacional das Medidas Socioeducativas em Meio Abeiro List of cases involving the execution of socio-educational measures in the competent courts - 200Z.

ANNEX II

GROWTH RATES OF RESTRICTION AND PRIVATION OF LIBERTY - relation between 2009 *and* 2010

	SUOV1S3	INTERNATION			INTERNATION PROVISIONAL			SEMI FREEDOM			TOTAL		
		2009	2010	RATE	2009	2010	RATE	2009	2010	RATE	2009	2010	RATE
DEATH	AC	229	122	-46,72%	56	42	-25,00%	22	27	22,73%	307	191	-37,79%
	AP	51	31	-39,22%	39	40	2,56%	13	15	15,38%	103	86	-16,50%
	AM	05	33	-49,23%	18	25	38,89%	11	9	-18,18%	94	67	-28,72%
	PA	131	161	22,90%	77	94	22,08%	40	34	-15,00%	246	289	16,53%

	RO	195	169	-13,33%	19	19	0,00%	1	1	0,00%	215	189	-12,09%
	RR	14	10	-28,57%	15	13	-13,33%	9	6	-33,33%	38	29	-23,68%
	TO	51	80	56,86%	9	20	122,22%	22	23	4,55%	82	123	50,00%
NORTHEAST	AL	87	116	33,33%	26	39	50,00%	16	6	-62,50%	129	161	24,81%
		188	278	47,87%	114	123	7,89%	7	64	814,29%	309	465	50,49%
		615	646	5,04%	247	323	30,77%	BI	105	29,63%	943	1074	13,89%
		46	43	-6,52%	37	46	24,32%	19	17	-10,53%	102	106	3,92%
		223	151	-32,29%	16	49	206,25%	8	12	50,00%	247	212	-14,17%
	BA	1002	1023	2,10%	330	264	-20,00%	139	169	21,58%	1471	1456	-1,02%
	EC MA PB	48	57	18,75%	33	2	-93,94%	15	0	-100,00%	96	59	-38,54%
	PE PI RN	145	82	-43,45%	35	27	-22,86%	19	21	10,53%	199	130	-34,67%
	SE	73	76	4,11%	44	38	-13,64%	22	27	22,73%	139	141	1,44%
WEST CENTRE	DF	383	500	30,55%	143	173	20,98%	73	81	10,96%	599	754	25,88%
	GO	147	159	8,16%	108	69	-36,11%	9	11	22,22%	264	239	-9,47%
	MT	187	143	-23,53%	46	72	56,52%	0	0	0,00%	233	215	-7,73%
	MS	149	164	10,07%	46	27	-J1,30%	10	2	-80,00%	205	193	-5,85%
SOUTHEAST	ES	324	279	-13,89%	108	166	53,70%	11	14	27,27%	443	459	3,61%
	MG	764	652	-14,66%	222	284	27,93%	154	105	-31,82%	1140	1041	-8,68%
	RJ	303	344	13,53%	182	259	42,31%	148	230	55,41%	633	633	31,60%
	SP	4769	5107	7,09%	957	1168	22,05%	500	539	7,80%	6226	6814	9,44%
SOUTH	PR SC	701	778	10,98%	201	253	25,87%	66	52	-21,21%	968	1083	11,88%
	RS BR	164	168	2,44%	223	193	-13,45%	111	73	-34,23%	498	434	-12,85

												%
	847	669	-21,02% 1,18%	120	106	-11,67% 13,34%	42	85	102,38% 10,20%	1009	860	-14,77% 4,50%

ANNEX III

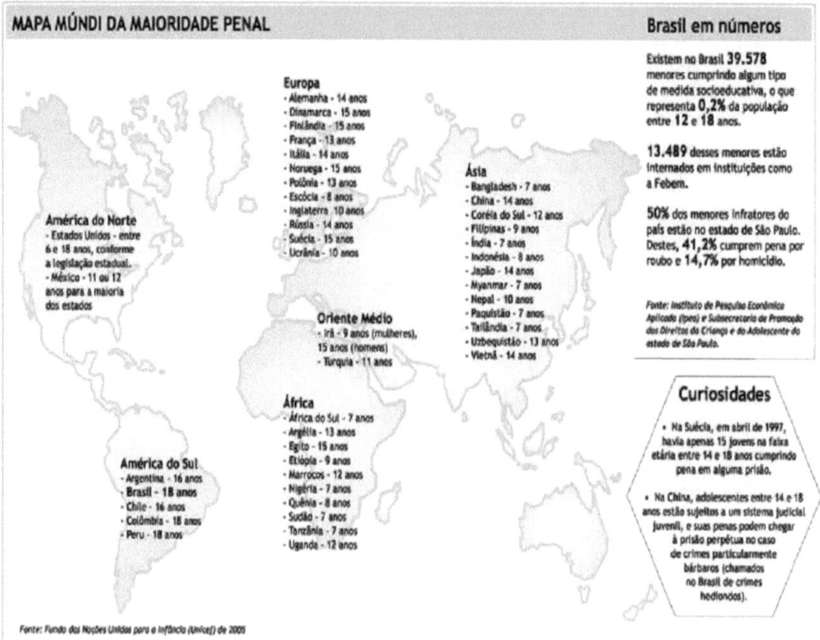

BILIOGRAPHICAL REFERENCES

ALVES, Roberto Barbosa. **Childhood and youth law.** São Paulo: Saraiva, 2005.

BARROS, Flávio Monteiro de. **Criminal law:** general part. 7. ed. São Paulo: Saraiva, 2009.

BITENCOURT, Cezar Roberto. **Criminal law manual:** general part. 7. ed. rev. and updated. São Paulo: Saraiva, 2002.

BITTAR, Eduardo Carlos Bianca. **Methodology of legal research.** São Paulo: Saraiva, 2001.

BONFIM, Edilson Mougenot; CAPEZ, Fernando. **Criminal law:** general part. São Paulo: Saraiva,

2004.

BRAZIL. **Explanatory memorandum to the new general part of the penal code.** Law no. 7.209, of 11 July 1984.

BRAZIL. **Law No. 8.069, of 13 July 1990.** Provides for the Statute of the Child and Adolescent.

BRAZIL. **Proposed amendment to the constitution No. 83 of 2011.** Available at: <http://www.senado.gov.br/atividade/materia/getPDF.asp?t=95505&tp=l>. Accessed on: 11 September 2011.

CANADIAN CENTRE FOR JUSTICE STATISTICS. **A profile of young justice in Canada.** Ottawa: Minister of Industry Canada, 1998.

CAPEZ, Fernando. **The question of reducing the age of criminal responsibility.** Available at: <http://www.epm.sp.gov.br/Internas/ArtigosView.aspx?ID=3016>. Accessed on: 27 October 2010.

CAPEZ, Fernando. **Criminal law:** general part. 2. ed. São Paulo: Saraiva, 2001. v. 1.

CAVALLIERI, Alyrio. **Flaws in the Statute for Children and Adolescents.** Rio de Janeiro: Forense, 1995.

PEOPLE'S MAIL. **Justice surprises and applies light sentence to rapists in SC.** Available at: <htpp://www.correiodopovo.com.br/Noticias/?Noticia=181771>. Accessed on: 08 September 2011.

COSTA JÚNIOR, Paulo José da. **Comentários ao código penal.** 6. ed. current. São Paulo: Saraiva, 2009.

COUTINHO, Luiz Augusto. **Retrograde step of reducing criminal imputability to 16 years.** Available at: <http://jus.uol.com.br/revista/texto/4218/retrocesso-da-reducao-da- imputabilidade-penal-para-16-anos>. Accessed on: 28 August 2011.

CURY, Munir. (Coord.) **Estatuto da criança e do adolescente comentado.** 7. ed. São Paulo: Malheiros, 2005.

CURY, Munir. (Coord.) **Estatuto da criança e do adolescente comentado.** 10. ed. São Paulo: Malheiros, 2010.

DA SILVA, José Afonso. **Contextual commentary on the constitution.** 5. ed. São Paulo: Malheiros, 2008.

DOTTI, René Ariel. **Criminal law course:** general part. Rio de Janeiro: Forense, 2001.

DOTTI, René Ariel. **Criminal law course:** general part. Rio de Janeiro: Forense, 2005.

EBADI, Shirin. Interview. **Lawyer's Journal.** São Paulo. Year XXXVII. n. 363, July 2011. Available at: <htpp://www2.oabsp.org.br/asp//jomal/defaut.asp>. Accessed on: 23 August 2011.

ÉDER, Jorge. **Reducing the age of criminal responsibility.** Available at: <http://jus.uol.com.br/revista/texto/3374/reducao-da-maioridade-penal>. Accessed on: 27 August 2011.

FERRANDIN, Mauro. **Ato infracional:** aplicabilidade dos princípios e garantias do ato penal. Curitiba: Juruá, 2009.

FRANCO, Alberto Silva; NUCCI, Guilherme de Souza. (**Criminal Law.** São Paulo: Revista dos Tribunais, 2010. v. 7.

GERRAUD, René. **Compendium of criminal law.** Campinas: LZN, 2003. vol. 1.

GUERREIRO, Gabriela. **President of the Supreme Court says he is against reducing the age of criminal responsibility.** Available at: <http://wwwl.folha.uol.com.br/cotidiano/ult95ul31528.shtml>. Accessed on 28 August 2011.

HOLTHE, Leo Van. **Constitutional Law.** 5 ed. revised, updated. Salvador: Jus Podivm, 2009.

HOUSE OF LORDS. Parliamentary business. Publications & records. Lords publications. **Judgement Index.** Available at: <http://www.publications.parliament.uk/pa/ld200809/ldjudgmt/jd090429/jtb-l.htm>. Accessed on: 08 September 2011.

BRAZILIAN INSTITUTE OF GEOGRAPHY AND STATISTICS. **Channels:** States@: São Paulo. Available at: <http://www.ibge.gov.br/estadosat/perfil.php?sigla=sp>. Accessed on: 07 May 2011.

BRAZILIAN INSTITUTE OF GEOGRAPHY AND STATISTICS. **Population:** 2010 Census. Available at: <http://www.ibge.gov.br/home/presidencia/noticias/noticia_vizualiza.php?id_noticia=1766>. Accessed on: 07 May 2011.

UNITED NATIONS LATIN AMERICAN INSTITUTE FOR THE PREVENTION OF CRIME AND TREATMENT OF OFFENDERS. **National mapping of open-ended socio-educational measures:** summary report. 2010. Available at: <http://www.ilanud.org.br/midia/doc/relatorio_resumido_mapeamento_mse_abr2009.pdf>. Accessed on 09 July 2011.

JESUS, Damásio E. de. **Criminal law:** general part. 31. ed. São Paulo: Saraiva, 2010. v. 1.

LENZA, Pedro. **Direito Constitucional esquematizado.** 12. ed. rev., atual, e ampl. São Paulo: Saraiva, 2008.

NATIONAL SURVEY: Socio-educational Assistance for Adolescents in Conflict with the Law 2010. Available at: <http://www.viablog.org.br/conteudo/LEVANTAMENTO_Socioed.pdf>. Accessed on: 09 July 2011.

MAHER, Gerry. Age and criminal responsibility. **Ohio State Journal of Criminal Law,** Columbus. Available at: <htpp://moritzlaw.osu.edu/osjcl/Articles/V olume2_2/Symposium/Maher-PDF-4-l 1 -O5.pdf>. Accessed on: 19 August 2011.

MARTINS, Ives Granda da Silva; MENDES, Gilmar Ferreira; DO NASCIMENTO, Carlos Valder. **Treatise on constitutional law.** São Paulo: Saraiva, 2010.

MARTINS, Ives Granda; REZEK, Francisco (Coord.). **Federal Constitution:** advances, contributions and changes in the Brazilian democratic process. São Paulo: Ed. Revista dos Tribunais: University Extension Centre, 2008.

MENDEZ, Emílio Garcia; DA COSTA, Antônio Carlos Gomes. **From needs to rights.** São Paulo: Malheiros, 1994.

MIRABETE, Júlio Fabbrini. **Manual of criminal law:** general part. 24. ed. rev. and updated. São Paulo: Atlas, 2008. vol. 1.

MIRABETE, Júlio Fabbrini. **Manual of criminal law:** general part. 25. ed. rev. and updated. São Paulo: Atlas, 2009. vol. 1.

MONTEIRO, André. **Brazil's prisons and criminal justice system dysfunctional, says report.** Available at: <http://wwwl .folha.uol.com.br/folha/cotidiano/ult95u722246.shtml>. Accessed on 24 September 2011.

MOREIRA, Fabrício Calado. **Federal government has increased spending, but some social problems have been reduced, says IPEA.** Available at: <htpp://noticias.uol.com.br/política/2011/08/25/govemo-federal-a aumento-gastos-bas- programas-social-tiveram-reducao-diz-ipea.jhtm>. Accessed on 26 August 2011.

NOGUEIRA, Paulo Lúcio. **Commentary on the juvenile code.** 3. ed. São Paulo: Saraiva, 1987.

NORONHA, E. Magalhães. **Criminal Law:** introduction and general part. 38. ed. revised and updated. São Paulo: Saraiva, 2004. v. 1.

NUCCI, Guilherme de Souza. **Commentary on the Criminal Code.** 9. ed. rev., atual, e ampl. São Paulo: Revista dos Tribunais, 2008.

NUCCI, Guilherme de Souza. **Criminal law manual:** general and special parts. 6. rev. ed. updated and expanded. São Paulo: Revista dos Tribunais, 2009.

OLIVEIRA, José Carlos de. (Org.) **Temas** de **direito público.** Jaboticabal: Funep, 2009.

PAGNAN, Rogério. **STF president compares prisons to dungeons** . Available at: <htpp://wwwl. folha, uol.com.br/cotidiano/894132-presidente-do-stf-compara-prisoes-a- masmorras-medievais.shtml>. Accessed on: 24 September 2011.

PEREIRA, Tânia da Silva. **Direito da criança e do adolescente:** uma proposta interdisciplinar. 2. ed. rev. e atual. Rio de Janeiro: Renovar, 2008.

RAMIDOFF, Mário Luiz. **Lições de direito da criança e do adolescente.** 2. ed. rev. e atual. Curitiba: Juruá, 2011.

REBELO, Carlos Eduardo Barreiros. **The age of criminal majority and the controversy over its reduction.** Belo Horizonte: Jus, 2010.

LEGAL JOURNAL OF THE FEDERAL UNIVERSITY OF PARANÁ. Curitiba, n. 49, 2009.

LEGAL JOURNAL OF THE UNIVERSITY OF FRANCA. Franca, year 4, n.6, 2001.

RIPOLLES, A. Quintano. **Comentários al código penal.** Madrid: Revista del Derecho Privado Madrid, 1966.

ROXIN, Claus. **Derecho penal parte general:** Tomo I. Fundamentals. The structure of criminal theory. Madrid: Thomson Civitas, 2003.

SALLA, Thiago Mio; LEOMIL, Leonardo. **Experts question the reduction of the age of criminal responsibility.** Available at: <http://www.4usp.usp.br/index.php/ciencias/11142>. Accessed on 27 October 2010.

SARAIVA, João Batista Costa. **Compendium of juvenile criminal law:** adolescents and offences. 3. ed., rev. and expanded. Porto Alegre: Livraria do Advogado, 2006.

STÊNCIO, Renata Franchi. **The age of majority:** a political and legal choice. 2008. 66 f. Final Coursework. (Law degree). Faculty of History, Law and Social Work, Universidade Estadual Paulista "Júlio de Mesquita Filho", Franca, 2008.

STF, **Supreme Federal Court.** Available at: <http://www.stf.jus.br>. Accessed on: 23 June 2011.

TELES, Ney Moura. **Criminal Law:** general part - arts. I° to 120. São Paulo: Atlas, 2004. v.l.

UNICEF. **United Nations guidelines for the prevention of juvenile delinquency.** Available at:

<http://www.mp.rs.gov.br/infancia/documentos_intemacionais/idl 03,htm>. Accessed on 23 August 2011.

UNICEF. **Special Protections Progress & Disparity:** Old enough to be a criminal? Available at: <http://www.unicef.org/pon97/p56a.htm>. Accessed on: 19 August 2011.

MIX
Papier aus verantwortungsvollen Quellen
Paper from responsible sources
FSC® C105338

Printed by Books on Demand GmbH, Norderstedt / Germany